Jillian Harris   Tori Wesszer

FRAICHE FOOD, FULL HEARTS

A Collection of Recipes
for Every Day and Casual Celebrations

PENGUIN

an imprint of Penguin Canada, a division of Penguin Random House Canada Limited

Canada • USA • UK • Ireland • Australia • New Zealand • India • South Africa • China

First published 2019

www.penguinrandomhouse.ca

Library and Archives Canada Cataloguing in Publication

Title: Fraiche food, full hearts : a collection of recipes for every day and casual celebrations / Jillian Harris, Tori Wesszer.
Names: Harris, Jillian, author. | Wesszer, Tori, author.
Identifiers: Canadiana (print) 20190046821 | Canadiana (ebook) 20190046848 | ISBN 9780735234307
(hardcover) | ISBN 9780735234314 (PDF)
Subjects: LCSH: Cooking. | LCGFT: Cookbooks.
Classification: LCC TX714 .H37 2019 | DDC 641.5—dc23

Cover and book design by Kelly Hill
Cover and interior photography by Janis Nicolay
Food and prop styling by Jillian Harris, Tori Wesszer, Janis Nicolay, and Team Jilly

Printed and bound in the USA

10 9 8 7 6 5

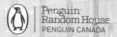

Penguin
Random House
PENGUIN CANADA

CONTENTS

This cookbook is for our sweet granny, Marjorie,
the Beet Roll Queen, who has always been the heart of our family
and is responsible for the Ukrainian recipes in this cookbook.
Her incredible love of food, laughter, and family will forever inspire
us. Thank you, Granny, for giving us the gift of cooking, being
the coolest grandma *ever*, and for loving us with all your heart.
We love you to the moon and back.

INTRODUCTION

Most people think we are sisters, but the truth is we are cousins—our moms are sisters. We grew up spending every possible moment together, going on any crazy adventure we could, and forever trying to match each other, from coordinated socks to matching yellow bikinis.

Our childhood was awesome. We were both very responsible kids and mature for our age, so we were given a lot of liberty. It was a bit crazy! Once, when Tori was sixteen (the ink on her driver's licence was still wet) and Jillian was fourteen, we went camping *by ourselves* in Tori's mom's mini van. Leaving from a family reunion in northern Alberta, we spent a week camping our way through the Rockies with a tent. Of course, that was long before cell phones, and we were too young for credit cards, so we relied on a bit of cash and a few pay phones to call home here and there to let everyone know we were still alive. We were nearly eaten by a bear in Banff, and Tori saved Jillian from choking on a tomato during a giggling fit (good thing for the Heimlich manoeuvre!), but we had so much fun.

Fast-forward to the present and we are still attached at the hip, living a stone's throw from each other, both bloggers and moms to our sweet kids (who are nearly identical ages). Our relationship is so special; we are seriously two lucky gals. This book offers a peek into our lives and the recipes that have fed our families through the years.

As with most families, our celebrations revolve around food; it is serious business over here. Our granny is the head honcho and is always the first one on the phone delegating dishes and overcommitting herself to cooking a feast. We grew up in a Ukrainian-dominated culture where fresh, seasonal veggies weren't exactly the highlight at mealtime. Holiday meals meant cabbage rolls, beet rolls, perogies, creamed mushrooms, turkey, gravy, stuffing, fluffy white buns, and green jellied salad (which clearly doesn't qualify as a "green," and don't worry, it didn't make the cut for this cookbook). Minutes before everyone sat down at the table, someone would throw a bowl of canned corn and some steamed peas on the table in between the bowl of sour cream and the dish of butter as a somewhat guilt-induced afterthought. Sigh.

We would love to say that we raised our own chickens and made our own almond milk in our spare time, but that would be a big fat lie. We were a typical family of the '80s. Processed foods were a routine part of our diet, and we never questioned where our food was from or what was in it.

Fortunately, our Ukrainian granny instilled the love of cooking in us at an early age. But family meals have become a bit trickier since we were kids! Two of our family members have celiac disease and can't eat gluten, a couple of us have turned to a more plant-based diet and have all but eliminated animal products, at least one person is on a low-carb kick at any given time, and of course we have picky kids in the mix. We swear if someone develops a nut allergy, they'll be kicked out of the family!

We suspect that our crew is not all that unique. Cooking for a crowd is tough to begin with, but cooking for a crowd with so many different food needs is enough to drive a person crazy! We wanted to find a way to help people create dishes for gatherings big or small, as well as everyday meals that can be easily adapted to fit everyone's requirements. Family meals are important, and so is your sanity. Let's face it, there's only so much wine a person can drink. (We would know, for the record.)

We eat for so many different reasons. The most obvious is to nourish ourselves and our families. But culture also determines what we eat, and it has really shaped this cookbook for us. Meals that speak to the heart, those nostalgic dishes from our childhood: we include a lot of these in the book. Wherever possible we lightened up these dishes to make them healthier and more earth-friendly by adapting them to be gluten-free or vegan (at the risk of getting an earful from our eighty-six-year-old granny and every other baba in the world!), but in a few cases we left them in all of their decadent glory.

We made a conscious effort to make this book as plant-heavy as we could, and focused on providing plant-based substitutions where meat or dairy was used traditionally. There is zero downside to eating more plants and fewer animal products. It is better for the environment (it takes fewer resources to produce plant-based foods versus animal-based foods), kinder to the animals (for obvious reasons), and better for our health—a serious win all round. There is a misconception that plant-based eating is expensive, lacks taste, or is difficult, but we promise it is none of these. If you are new to plant-based eating, please try some of the recipes with the plant-based substitutions. We bet you will be pleasantly surprised!

We wrote this cookbook together, but since we are different people with our own perspectives, here are a few thoughts from each of our desks.

Note from Jillian

I was not always a whiz in the culinary department. My earliest memory of getting creative in the kitchen involves some very pasty blueberry muffins that I made at the ripe age of five while my parents had a meeting with some kind of financial guy. I put on my apron, added some blueberries to some flour, sugar, and milk, mixed it all up, and popped it in the oven. Six minutes later, voila—fresh and soggy blueberry muffins were served. The meeting must not have been a successful one because my parents nicely declined the muffins but urged the financial guy to eat one. Poor guy. I remember tasting one and thinking, *These are horrible!*

I always loved being in the kitchen and experimenting. At a young age I was the lucky recipient of one of those mini stoves many kids in the '80s had. They were stoves that you could actually bake in. We kept ours in the basement playroom, sitting right on the carpet—talk about a liability! I recall Tori came around to play one day and she was so excited about giving it a shot. To my horror, I had forgotten about some garlic bread I'd made a few weeks earlier. Inside my little oven it had turned into a petri dish of garlicky mould.

Okay, so I did not always have the magic touch in the kitchen, but I was never afraid to try new things and experiment. I had an odd palate for a kid, starting from when I was four. One of my favourite dishes was mushrooms stuffed with escargots, and I loved onion sandwiches, Marmite, pickled eggs, and pickled herring. I would try *anything* anyone offered me.

Some of my fondest memories in the kitchen involve Christmases at Tori's parents' place. Tori and I helped with Christmas baking and Christmas dinner and wanted to be a part of it from start to finish. I am not sure if we were actually much help or if we just drove our moms crazy, but I remember spending a ton of time in the kitchen. My mom and grandma were my biggest culinary influences. They always encouraged me to be creative, try new things, and tweak recipes just to see what would happen. I still have the recipe for my and Grandma's Crazy Tomato Soup Cake that we created together.

My journey with food has taken quite a turn over the last few years. My favourite foods growing up may have included bacon, cream, butter, cheese, and sour cream, but over the years I have come to look at food differently and now have a new respect for where food comes from. I also feel strongly that one of the reasons I have a ring on my finger is because of my cooking. My fiancé, Justin, always talks about the *love weight* he gained in our first year together. He reminisces about the jar of bacon grease I would keep on the kitchen counter for cooking.

Although many of my readers on www.jillianharris.com think I am vegan, I am not, but I would say I am a much more conscious eater than I used to be. Do not get me wrong: a cheese perogy with fried bacon, onions, and sour cream is still one of my favourite dishes of all time, but nowadays I prefer plant-based foods and reduce the amount of animal products I consume. I prefer local and fresh ingredients wherever possible. I limit my consumption of animal products and only consume the absolute best local, small-farm, free-range, grass-fed, massaged, loved, sung-to animal products. (Believe it or not, my no-negotiation item is pork, so no more bacon for this gal!) What about Justin? Well, it took a year or two, but after reading enough articles and watching documentaries, the whole family has adopted the same eating style. Justin is always excited when I make a savoury, hot, comfort meal and tell him its vegan. He's up for trying anything new and has been enthusiastic about the change. Our son Leo's favourites include smoked tofu, baked beans, vegan bolognaise, and of course Tori's Angel Cakes. Our daughter Annie was born while wrapping up the final stages of our cookbook. We hope she will be an adventurous eater, too!

The focus on food has really changed in our house. We are always planning meals around what is in season, local, healthy, and good for the earth. And, of course, it has to be delicious! I realize this is a polarizing and controversial topic, but this cookbook is not about just me; it is about our family, the way we entertain, our traditions, our grandma and uncle Dougie's stubborn ways, and feeding the whole damn family. While I wish I could label this cookbook and my diet, there is no black-and-white way to put it. Tori and I have made most of our recipes thoughtful, vegetarian- or vegan-convertible, heavy on the plants, and easier on the environment.

In the end, what matters most to us is that you have fun with this cookbook, that we are all going back to putting down our devices, laughing, talking (not texting), cooking with each other, and creating memories. Because that is what really matters, right?

Jillian
xo

Note from Tori

Food has always been at the heart of our family, so it seems natural that when it was time for me to gravitate toward a profession, it was in the direction of food. Being in the kitchen has always been my happy place. And since Jillian and I were joined at the hip growing up, we ended up spending a good chunk of our childhood together in the kitchen having the time of our lives creating new things, some edible, some not! Little did we know that this early love of cooking and baking, along with the creative freedom our parents let us have in the kitchen (we made a lot of big messes to go with those sometimes questionable dishes), would set the foundation for our cookbook.

When I was growing up, I assumed that all families were like Jillian's and mine. We all live within a stone's throw of each other, have the whole crew on speed dial, and celebrate every single holiday together. It isn't always fancy (actually, it rarely is) or even totally civil (we're family, after all), but it's my kind of perfect. I think it was a bit of a shock for my husband, Charles, when he entered the family without reading the fine print: you sign up for the group deal with our clan! I love them all to bits and am so grateful to have such a tight-knit family that can laugh and joke and tease each other and always know that we have each other's backs. It has had a profound influence over who I am today, on for how I want to raise Max and Charlie now that I'm a mom. Family really means everything to Charles and me, and we want our boys to grow up having that same bond with their cousins, aunts, and uncles. It's my life goal to give them the same magical Christmas mornings and mind-bending Easter egg hunts that we had growing up.

I have loved baking ever since I was about five years old according to my mom, but if my memory serves me correctly, I have not always been good at it. The first loaf of bread I ever baked easily weighed a solid ten pounds, and our dog would not even touch the first pie I made. Ouch. They say that practice makes perfect, and here I am, still practising away.

I have always been completely obsessed with cookbooks. I used to copy out recipes in perfectly neat handwriting on index cards and file them away in an accordion folder that I still have (I'd like those hours back for the record!). I read cookbooks the way most people read novels. But I never thought I would be lucky enough to write a cookbook of my own, especially with my "sister"—it's a dream come true!

I took an interest in nutrition at an early age. I think it started in grade five, when we learned about the difference between white bread and brown bread and a million reasons to eat your veggies, and I was hooked. My poor parents! Honestly, I think I turned into their biggest nightmare. I took it a bit far, to be honest, forgetting to recognize that food serves a number of purposes in our lives beyond providing nutrients, and that there was still a place for the food that we grew up with, as rich as it may have been. Now that I have my own family, I want Max and Charlie to grow up with a healthy relationship with food. We talk a lot about "sometimes foods" and "everyday foods," and how they can both fit in a well-rounded diet. I am not vegan but have always eaten a plant-heavy diet, and I'm always looking for new ways to make plant-based eating, and food in general, more enjoyable.

So here's the deal. The dietitian in me wants to tell you that some of the recipes in this book are "sometimes foods" that we eat in moderation on special occasions. However, the foodie in me wants to pour you a good glass of wine and tell you that life is short and eating dishes made from quality ingredients, in moderation and in good company, is totally okay. I think both perspectives are right. I grew up with perogies and have zero intention of giving them up the few times a year that I eat them. Food is meant to be nourishing in every sense of the word. Yes, we need to feed our body with the nutrients it needs to be strong and healthy. But I also believe that food, preferably home-cooked with incredible wholesome ingredients (and mostly plants), is meant to be enjoyed with friends and family in all of its nostalgic glory to nourish our souls as well. Because food is love.

We are so honoured to be able to share this labour of love and little piece of our family with you. We wrote this cookbook with the hope that it will help inspire you to eat together more often, cook your own food using beautiful, simple, wholesome ingredients, eat more plants, indulge a little when it counts, and most important, to have fun with those you love.

Tori
xo

About This Book

Fraiche Food, Full Hearts includes over 100 recipes that we have grown to love over the years. Some have roots in our childhood, recipes passed down through generations with the best memories attached to them, like long lazy afternoons making perogies at the table with our granny. We realized that many of these family recipes had never actually been written down! Others have been brought into the fold along the way, like our Roasted Root Veggie Soup (page 143) that we used to eat together snuggled under a blanket on cold, rainy Vancouver nights when we were single and lived across the street from each other. Jillian and I are grateful to be able to capture them all here, sharing with you the recipes for dishes that fed us through our childhood and beyond.

Our granny has always been at the centre of it all and has inspired us through the years to roll up our sleeves and dig in. In doing so, it has brought us closer together as a family. Let's face it, when you ask people to come for dinner, they usually come (especially when Granny is cooking!). Our meals are always super casual, family style, with jokes being cracked non-stop as the dishes are devoured, sometimes with a bit of competition involved. In our family, Granny's Beet Rolls (page 249) are the best test of survival of the fittest: if you're not fast, you get *none*; if you take the last one . . . watch your back! We know that these shared meals are a big reason why we are such a tight-knit family, and we would not have it any other way. Our fun and crazy family gatherings are what inspired us to create the celebration menus in this book.

This cookbook is organized into familiar categories of breakfasts, appetizers and snacks, salads and soups, main dishes, veggies and sides, and desserts. Our recipes can be made at any time of the year for any occasion, including everyday meals. The recipes are mostly vegetarian; there are some fish and seafood dishes, but the majority are plant-based, which is typically how we eat.

We have included a section that discusses our preferences in frequently used ingredients as well as how to source the best food possible. We also share our list of our go-to pantry staples and kitchen tools that we use regularly to help you get set up in your own kitchen.

At the beginning of each recipe, we have included dietary indicators:

VEGAN The recipe does not contain any animal products such as meat, eggs, fish, dairy, or honey.

VEGETARIAN The recipe does not contain any meat, chicken, or fish, but may contain dairy products or eggs.

DAIRY-FREE The recipe does not contain dairy products.

GLUTEN-FREE The recipe does not contain any gluten. Some ingredients that you would normally think of as being gluten-free, such as oats and even coconut, may be manufactured in facilities where cross-contamination can occur. It is therefore important to use certified gluten-free ingredients when you are cooking for someone who is gluten-sensitive or who has celiac disease.

NUT-FREE The recipe does not include any tree nuts. Double-check ingredient labels if you are cooking for someone who has a nut allergy, as cross-contamination can occur during production.

In most recipes we've given suggestions to make them vegan, and in some to make them gluten-free. We put these modifications at the bottom of the page. We know first-hand how diverse a family can be when it comes to food, so we have labelled all our recipes to help accommodate different dietary needs.

About the Ingredients

Ingredients matter. We have started to be more mindful of our environment and the impact that our food choices have on the planet. Too many of us today are disconnected from our food supply, and therefore we are shielded from the fact that some foods have made a "nicer" journey to our plates than others. We are not suggesting that everyone become a vegan (neither of us are completely vegan, for the record), but what we *are* suggesting is that you give a bigger portion of your plate to plants and be aware of where your food comes from. For starters, hit up farmers' markets to support your community and have access to the *best* food you will ever buy. If you choose to still eat eggs, buy free-range (cage-free) eggs. Better yet, buy your eggs straight from the farmer, at farmers' markets or even from the farm itself, where you can see the chickens running around. If you eat meat, try to find a butcher that sources from farms that treat their animals ethically and don't use hormones and antibiotics, and try to cut back on your portions as much as possible. If this concept is new to you, why not experiment with a Meatless Monday, or try out plant-based alternatives to animal products even when a recipe is not completely plant-based. All we are suggesting is that you lean into eating more plants in any way you can. It all counts. We promise you, your body and the earth will be so grateful you did! On the following page are some notes on ingredients commonly used throughout this book.

SALT We typically use fine sea salt in our recipes, but kosher salt is a good choice as well. Fleur de sel or flaked salt like Maldon is also great to have on hand for finishing dishes.

FLOUR When a recipe calls for all-purpose flour, we use unbleached.

OIL Extra-virgin olive oil is our preference, but because it has a distinct flavour, it is not suitable for some recipes. Avocado oil is a good choice for frying at high heat, is neutral in taste, and has a healthy fatty acid profile, but other neutral vegetable oils, such as grapeseed oil or canola oil, will work as well. When a recipe calls for coconut oil, we use virgin coconut oil (not the unflavoured kind).

BUTTER When vegan butter is called for, we use the stick version. If you do choose to use butter, we recommend buying good-quality organic grass-fed unsalted butter made by a local dairy.

CREAM Many of our family dishes were prepared using cream, but we substituted our own Cashew Cream (page 313) as a healthier plant-based option with major success! We love cashew cream for

its super-creamy texture and because it's so easy to make it yourself in a blender (bonus: you do not need to strain it).

MILK We use unsweetened almond milk in many of our recipes, although other milks will work just as well. Many of our family recipes were originally made with cow's milk, but for all of the reasons we have mentioned we have done our best to give plant-based alternatives that do not compromise the quality of the dish. Where coconut milk is called for we use canned, full-fat coconut milk.

BOUILLON AND STOCK We use bouillon and stock in our recipes to add flavour, and we've discovered a couple of amazing vegetable-based concentrated versions that come in a jar and are easily reconstituted. You may have to hunt for them, but it's worth the effort. They eliminate the need to cart around heavy containers of stock (and are better for the environment since all that water is saved from being shipped across the miles), and you can make exactly what you need for a given recipe. We have fallen in love with the Better Than

Bouillon brand's vegetarian line. They come in chicken and beef flavours and are awesome for giving a plant-based dish the same taste as the real deal. They are high in sodium, though, so you may find dishes don't need any extra salt.

EGGS We use large free-range eggs in our recipes. We encourage you to source local eggs if you can.

SUGAR We use organic white cane sugar when a recipe calls for sugar. You can substitute the same amount of coconut sugar in most recipes, though the taste will not be identical.

HONEY We use liquid honey (not creamed, unless it's called for) and only buy locally sourced honey that is ethically harvested—not the big tubs of honey you find in most grocery stores. Maple syrup can be substituted in most cases.

MAYONNAISE We tested all our recipes with vegan mayonnaise. There are some very good brands available. A traditional mayonnaise will work just as well, but come on, after all we've said, why not use a plant-based one?

Kitchen and Pantry Staples

A well-stocked pantry and kitchen will make a world of difference to your cooking game. Here are some of the pantry staples, kitchen tools, and small appliances that we highly recommend you keep on hand.

FATS

Extra-virgin olive oil
Avocado oil
Grapeseed oil
Vegan butter (sticks)
Virgin coconut oil
Sesame oil
Vegetable oil

NUTS, SEEDS & BUTTERS

(We buy these at the bulk food store, where they are most economical.)
Raw cashews
Raw almonds
Sliced raw almonds
Raw pecans
Walnuts
Chia seeds
Ground flaxseed
Sesame seeds
Pumpkin seeds
Sunflower seeds
Hemp seeds
Almond butter
Tahini

CANNED & BOTTLED GOODS

Vegetarian stock concentrates (we like the Better Than Bouillon brand vegetarian beef-flavoured and chicken-flavoured versions)
Vegetable stock
Beans (black beans, chickpeas, kidney beans)
Full-fat coconut milk and coconut cream
Corn kernels
Diced tomatoes
Fire-roasted whole tomatoes
Tomato paste
Soy sauce
Tamari
Hot sauce
Chipotle peppers in adobo sauce
Vinegar (black rice vinegar, white wine vinegar, red wine vinegar, white vinegar, apple cider vinegar)

SPICES

(Purchase spices in small amounts to keep them as fresh as possible.)
Allspice (ground)
Black pepper (ground)
Cayenne pepper
Chili powder
Cinnamon (ground and sticks)
Cumin (ground)
Dried oregano
Garlic powder
Ginger (ground and fresh)
Nutmeg (ground)
Onion powder
Paprika (sweet)
Salt (sea salt, table salt, fleur de sel)
Turmeric

SWEETENERS

Pure maple syrup
Pure liquid honey (preferably local)
Medjool dates
Brown sugar
White organic cane sugar
Coconut sugar

REFRIGERATED ITEMS

Fresh cilantro
Fresh flat-leaf parsley
Fresh basil
Fresh rosemary
Fresh sage
Extra-firm tofu
Herb or garlic cashew cheese
Almond milk (unsweetened, plain and vanilla flavoured)
Soy milk (unsweetened, plain and vanilla flavoured)
Mayonnaise (vegan)
Dijon mustard
Capers
Dill pickles

FROZEN ITEMS

Frozen corn
Frozen peas
Dairy-free vanilla ice cream
Coconut whipped topping

DRY GOODS

Nutritional yeast
Dry yeast (fast-rising and active dry)
Pasta (capellini, orzo, linguine, and any other shape you love)
Green lentils
Quinoa
Spring wheat kernels
Old-fashioned rolled oats
Flour (unbleached all-purpose and whole wheat)
Gluten-free I:I flour blend (if gluten-free required)
Baking powder
Baking soda
Rice (jasmine and brown)
Dutch-processed cocoa powder
Coconut (unsweetened shredded)
Coconut ribbons (from the bulk store)
Cornstarch
Panko crumbs
Dried cranberries
Raisins (we use Thompson)

WINE

(We live in wine country, so wine is a big deal in our neck of the woods! When cooking, only use wine you would drink! We used Sandhill wines in all of our recipes but substitute a different brand of the same varietal if Sandhill wines aren't available in your area. The varietals used are mentioned in the specific recipes.)
Dry red wine
Dry white wine

BAKING TOOLS

Rolling pin
Large baking sheets
Springform pan (9-inch/2.5 L)
Loaf pan
Muffin tin
13- × 9-inch (3 L) ceramic or glass baking dish
8-inch (2 L) square and round cake pans
Spring-release cookie scoops in various sizes
Kitchen scale
Parchment paper
Paper muffin liners
Aluminum foil

COOKING TOOLS

Chef's knife (the best you can afford): a 6-inch (15 cm) is our preference
Paring knife
Vegetable peeler
Garlic press
Heavy-bottomed pots
Cast-iron frying pan
Nonstick frying pans
High-speed blender
Immersion blender
Food processor (and a mini version)
Stand mixer
Hand-held electric mixer
Citrus juicer
Microplane zester
Colander and mesh sieve
Wooden spoons
Rubber spatulas
Wire whisk

CELEBRATION MENUS

Valentine's Day

We love the idea of celebrating Valentine's Day with one's sweetheart by candle light, with a nice bottle of red wine and a giant plate of spaghetti. However, we are possibly more excited about spending it lounging in bed with our bestie eating piles of fluffy pancakes washed down with some bubbly!

BESTIE BREAKFAST IN BED

Angel Cakes (page 63)
Tofu Veggie Scramble (page 73)
Sweetheart Oven Fries (page 77)
Champagne

ROMANTIC DINNER FOR TWO

Great Green Salad (page 135)
Pink Pasta (page 157)
Green Garlic Bread (page 94)
Black Bean Coconut Brownies (page 280; after baking cut them into heart shapes with a heart-shaped cookie cutter to up the adorable factor)

DINNER FOR A CROWD

(for those un-romantic Valentine's Days!)

Rosemary Polenta Fries with Smoky Tomato Dip (page 111)
Great Green Salad (page 135)
Tori's Thin Crust Pizza (page 201; make them in the shape of a heart
if you are ambitious)
Cherry Sweetheart Slab Pie (page 267)

Easter

**A**s kids, Easter was darned exciting. Tori's dad and Jillian's mom put their heads together every year, and without fail Bob and Peggy would create an incredible Easter egg hunt with hilarious little riddles along the way. We would find notes like "Great job, kids! Okay, now head on down to the tree that weeps, there you will find your next clue, you little creeps!" We really had to work for that basket of candy! As our own kids get older, this is 100 percent something we will be doing with them. It gave us the *best* memories!

In our family, Easter dinner is just like Christmas (and Thanksgiving)—we *all* celebrate together. Tables are dressed in pastels, and pretty spring flowers decorate the room. We usually do it potluck style, where everyone is responsible for bringing something (a smart idea, given that there are so many of us!). If you choose to cook a ham or turkey, try to source it from a local farm that treats their animals well.

EASTER BRUNCH

Aunty Mary's Banana Bread (page 289)

West Coast Eggs Benny (page 69)

Crispy Roasted Rosemary Potatoes (page 210)

Fresh fruit

Coffee

EASTER DINNER

Granny's Borscht (page 140)

Perfect White Buns (page 239)

Ukrainian Savoury Crepes (page 246)

Creamy Dill Mushrooms (page 213)

Maple Thyme Roasted Parsnips and Carrots (page 218)

Potato Garlic Cauliflower Mash (page 209)

Mushroom Wellington (page 177)

White wine

Mother's Day

**M**other's Day has grown into a more intimate holiday for us as our family has grown bigger, and now we tend to celebrate our own moms at our own homes. Peggy (Jillian's mom) and Patsy (Tori's mom) are two exceptional ladies. They are sisters but also closest friends who talk to each other every day. We can honestly say that we are who we are because of them. They are creative, kind, beautiful in every way, and super talented. We are so lucky to have them as our moms!

MOTHER'S DAY BRUNCH

Broiled Grapefruit with Coconut Almond Granola (page 81)

Tofu Veggie Scramble (page 73) or scrambled eggs

Angel Cakes (page 63)

Currant or Raisin Biscuits (page 235)

Coffee

Fresh-squeezed orange or grapefruit juice with a splash of Prosecco

MOTHER'S DAY DINNER

Smoked Salmon Cakes with Dill Tartar Sauce (page 121)

Spring Orecchiette (page 154)

Irish Apple Cake (page 255) with Vegan Caramel Sauce (page 256)

Strawberry Rosé-arita (page 296)

Father's Day

Our dads simply melt our hearts. Since our moms are sisters, what would be the chance that they would each marry the most awesome guys in the world who also love to hang out together? Each of our dads is a very funny guy, but when they are together, the "hilarious factor" is exponentially amplified; they absolutely feed off each other and have the whole room in stitches every single time!

Glen (Jilly's dad) and Bob (Tori's dad) are sweet, talented, generous, positive human beings who were the very best male influence we girls could ask for. It set the bar high for our future soulmates. Good thing we found our own diamonds in the rough: Justin and Charles are seriously the best dads and such incredible supportive partners. Oh yeah, and they are funny and basically BFFs too. How lucky are we!

Obviously, spoiling the men in our lives is important. And of course you know the way to a man's heart . . .

FATHER'S DAY BRUNCH

Breakfast Enchiladas (page 67)

Crispy Roasted Rosemary Potatoes (page 210)

Coffee

FATHER'S DAY DINNER

Captain's Kale Caesar Salad (page 131)

Rosemary Polenta Fries with Smoky Tomato Dip (page 111)

Garden Bolognese (page 158)

Green Garlic Bread (page 94)

Beer or red wine

or

Fresh Salsa and Guacamole (page 118) with tortilla chips

Mexican Kale Salad with Avocado Lime Dressing (page 139)

Big Burritos (page 203)

Grapefruit Jalapeño Margarita (page 302)

Garden Party

Summers in the Okanagan are pure perfection: we live for them. The evenings are warm until late in the night, and dinners al fresco are on repeat. Soft white lights are strung through fruit trees, rustic wooden tables are lined with organic linens, and glasses of crisp local white wine are our happy place. This is where life's magic happens.

Summer dinners are best when made with fresh local ingredients, usually from one of our gardens or the local farmers' market. The meal not only tastes better, but we get to support our local growers, which feels good!

GARDEN PARTY BRUNCH

Breakfast Bruschetta (page 67)

French Toast with Bourbon Peaches (page 64)

Vanilla Cherry Scones (page 83)

Fresh seasonal fruit

Okanagan Peach Slushies (page 295)

Iced coffee

GARDEN PARTY DINNER

Summer Squash Herb Tart (page 98)

Heirloom Tomato Fennel Panzanella (page 127)

Grilled Mexican Street Corn (page 217)

Cedar-Plank Salmon Burgers (page 197)

Peaches and Cream Shortcakes (page 263)

Cherry Sunset (page 299)

or

Great Green Salad (page 135)

Seafood "Bake" (page 189)

Cheddar Chive Biscuits (page 235)

Mini Cherry Almond Crumbles (page 279)

White wine

Birthday

obody knows how to do a birthday party like Jillian. She goes all out! There is no better way to celebrate someone than making a good homemade dinner—usually whatever that special person wants of course. Here are some of our go-to dishes when we want to spoil that special someone!

Sweet Chili Tofu (page 101)

Vegetarian Chili (page 184)

Skillet Cornbread (page 231)

Peggy's Chocolate Cake (page 260)

Beer or red wine

Rainbow Salad Rolls with Crispy Tofu (page 103)

Great Green Salad (page 135)

Lime Capellini (page 160)

Green Garlic Bread (page 94)

Naked Coconut Cake (page 265)

White wine

Thanksgiving

Thanksgiving dinner has always looked the same—until last year. We turned it all on its head by serving a completely vegan Thanksgiving feast. Turns out our family loves the side dishes more than the main: the turkey was not missed!

If a vegan Thanksgiving isn't your jam, may we suggest sourcing a turkey that comes from a local farm and has been raised ethically. Especially in the fall, farmers' markets are buzzing, and you can get more than just your turkey there. Yes, these birds are more expensive, but we promise that they are worth every penny. Here are a number of plant-based dishes to share with your crew to make yours the most delicious Thanksgiving yet! We love keeping it simple and natural, and have included suggestions for decorating a fall-inspired Thanksgiving table.

Table-Setting Suggestions

- Fresh apples (preferably with the leaves—they are so pretty)
- Small white pumpkins
- Candles in glass jars (you can even use mason jars)
- Thin branches with leaves on them (we love apple branches, but use whatever you can get your hands on)
- Gold or vintage cutlery
- Gold or pewter-coloured chargers
- Vintage silver platters
- White and gold place cards
- Linen napkins and tablecloth
- Little notes at each setting with the words "I'm thankful for . . ." Give everyone a pencil to jot down their thoughts and share at the dinner table.

THANKSGIVING DINNER

Harvest Kale Slaw with
Tahini Dressing (page 136)

Perfect White Buns (page 239)

Vegan Perogies (page 243)

Maple Thyme Roasted Parsnips and
Carrots (page 218)

Southern Pecan Sweet Potatoes
(page 221)

Mushroom Wellington (page 177)

Mushroom Gravy (page 229)

Potato Garlic Cauliflower Mash
(page 209)

Steamed green peas

Pecan Pumpkin Pie (page 272)

Christmas

C hristmas with our crew is really something else. In fact, we call it the "Hillbilly Christmas," and for good reason. Since we were little we have all celebrated Christmas together, and when we say "all," this includes cousins, aunts, uncles, Granny, us kids, dogs, and now our own little babes, all sleeping under the same roof. It is crazy and chaotic and we simply would not have it any other way. The Christmas tree is always overloaded, stockings are piled all over the place, and people are sleeping in every corner of the house. One year we even put the guys in Jillian's garage when they got too rowdy! We used to pile sleeping bags in the middle of the living room floor before all the kids had kids: it is truly magical waking up on Christmas morning to so much energy. Of course, the women are usually up until 4 a.m. wrapping gifts and drinking wine, with a massive dose of regret when the kids wake up at six!

The Christmas dinner table used to be filled with over-the-top rich Ukrainian dishes. While a lot of those dishes still grace the table (like Granny's Beet Rolls), we have added a ton of veggie dishes to the mix and have de-emphasized the meat. If you prefer to still have a turkey on the table, we highly recommend sourcing a smaller, locally raised bird that has come from a farm that treats their animals well. If you are looking for a heartier plant-based main, our go-to is Mushroom Wellington.

We love decorating the table for Christmas; on the next page we have included some suggestions to make your holiday table festive and gorgeous.

Table-Setting Suggestions

- Antique white or gold chargers topped with white plates
- Natural white or flax-coloured linens
- Plenty of white platters and bowls
- Twine with a sprig of rosemary to tie rolled napkins
- Loads of white candles in glass jars at different heights
- Cedar boughs and small berries
- Off-white roses
- Hand-written place cards

CHRISTMAS MORNING MENU

Ukrainian Christmas Wheat (Kutia)
with Poppy Seed Paste (page 89)

Paul's Bircher Muesli (page 78)

Tofu Veggie Scramble (page 73)

Sliced tomato

Cheddar Chive Biscuits (page 235) or toast

CHRISTMAS DINNER MENU

Roasted Root Veggies (page 222)

Vegan Perogies (page 243)

Perfect White Buns (page 239)

Granny's Beet Rolls (page 249)

Mushroom Wellington (page 177)

Mushroom Gravy (page 229)

Potato Garlic Cauliflower Mash (page 209)

Steamed green beans, peas, and/or corn

Jilly's Almost Famous Stuffing (page 227)

Sticky Apple Date Toffee Pudding (page 275)

Vegan Eggnog (page 309)

New Year's Eve

e have celebrated New Year's Eve so many different ways! Whether you are ringing in the New Year with a romantic dinner or kicking back around a campfire in plaid shirts, here are a couple of menus to help inspire you.

NEW YEAR'S APPETIZER BUFFET

Coconut Cauliflower Tacos with Pineapple Salsa (page 113)

Creamy Spinach and Artichoke Dip (page 108)

Sweet and Spicy Nuts (page 93)

Mini cups of Creamy Roasted Tomato Basil Soup with Garlic Croutons (page 148) or French Onion Soup with Thyme Croutons (page 144)

Butterless Butter Tart Squares (page 284)

Champagne

FANCY NEW YEAR'S DINNER

Mushroom Kale Garlic Toasts (page 97)

Terry's Big Mussels (page 122)

Potato-Crusted Halibut (page 198)

Garlicky Greens (page 214)

Irish Apple Cake (page 255) with Vegan Caramel Sauce (page 256)

Wine and champagne

RUSTIC NEW YEAR'S DINNER

Rosemary Polenta Fries with Smoky Tomato Dip (page 111)

Molasses Oatmeal Bread (page 233)

Granny's Overhauled Baked Beans (page 183)

Chewy Chocolate Chip Cookies (page 283)

Sammy's Mulled Wine (page 306)

BREAKFASTS

ANGEL CAKES

Makes 8 to 10 pancakes

These pancakes were nicknamed Angel Cakes by a family friend who fell in love with them when we made them on a camping trip. He ate *the whole batch*! These are light and fluffy and taste a million times better than any packaged mix. Regardless of the name, you will think you died and went to heaven! Our original recipe called for buttermilk, but we have substituted almond milk and lemon juice here. Omit the lemon juice or vinegar and use 2 cups (500 mL) of buttermilk if you want to stick with the original recipe. You can also substitute whole wheat flour for half, or all, of the all-purpose flour.

1. Preheat the oven to 200°F (100°C). Line a baking sheet with parchment paper.

2. Combine the almond milk with the lemon juice in a measuring cup. Stir, then let sit for 5 minutes.

3. In a large bowl, mix together the flour, sugar, baking powder, baking soda, and salt.

4. In a medium bowl, whisk together the eggs, then whisk in the almond milk mixture, butter, and vanilla. Add the egg mixture to the flour mixture and stir just until combined. Do not overmix.

5. Heat a small amount of vegetable oil in a griddle or large frying pan over medium heat. Add ⅓ cup (75 mL) of the batter for each pancake. Cook until bubbles appear on the surface of the pancakes, 3 to 4 minutes; peek at the underside to make sure it is nicely browned before flipping. Flip and continue to cook until golden brown on the bottom, 3 to 4 minutes more. Transfer pancakes to the baking sheet and keep warm in the oven while you cook the remaining pancakes. Serve the pancakes with butter (if using), maple syrup, and fresh berries.

VEGAN: Skip the eggs and use ¼ cup (60 mL) vegan butter and 3½ teaspoons (17 mL) baking power.

DAIRY-FREE: Use vegan butter instead of butter.

NUT-FREE: Use buttermilk, soy milk, or your favourite nut-free milk instead of almond milk.

2 cups (500 mL) unsweetened almond milk

2 tablespoons (30 mL) fresh lemon juice or white vinegar

2 cups (500 mL) all-purpose flour

¼ cup (60 mL) sugar

2½ teaspoons (12 mL) baking powder

½ teaspoon (2 mL) baking soda

½ teaspoon (2 mL) salt

2 eggs

3 tablespoons (45 mL) butter or vegan butter, melted and cooled

1 teaspoon (5 mL) pure vanilla extract

Vegetable oil, for cooking

For serving

Butter or vegan butter (optional)

Pure maple syrup

Fresh berries

FRENCH TOAST WITH BOURBON PEACHES

Serves 4

Thick slices of French toast topped with a sensational bourbon peach sauce that dreams are made of. Seriously, when you get your hands on ripe peaches at the height of summer, make this recipe! We love serving this for brunch for special guests (especially those from out of town, since fresh Okanagan peaches are such a treat). For such an impressive dish, this does not take a lot of effort, and it really highlights beautiful seasonal fruit.

1. MAKE THE BOURBON PEACHES In a deep, heavy-bottomed frying pan, combine the peaches, 2 tablespoons (30 mL) of the butter, brown sugar, bourbon, vanilla, and salt. Cook over medium heat, gently stirring and folding the peaches, until the mixture bubbles, the sugar is dissolved, and the sauce thickens slightly, 4 to 5 minutes.

2. Add the remaining 1 tablespoon (15 mL) butter and gently stir the peach mixture until the butter is melted and fully incorporated. Remove from the heat and set aside while you make the French toast.

3. Preheat the oven to 350°F (180°C).

4. MAKE THE FRENCH TOAST In a large, shallow bowl, whisk the eggs. Whisk in the almond milk, maple syrup, vanilla, cinnamon, and salt.

5. Heat 1 tablespoon (15 mL) of the butter and 1 tablespoon (15 mL) of avocado oil in a large nonstick frying pan over medium-low heat. Soak slices of the bread in the egg mixture for 30 seconds, coating on both sides. Cook the French toast in batches, being careful not to crowd the pan, until golden brown on both sides, 4 to 5 minutes per side.

6. Transfer the French toast to a baking dish, cover with foil, and keep warm in the oven. Repeat with the remaining bread slices, adding the remaining 1 tablespoon (15 mL) butter and 1 tablespoon (15 mL) avocado oil to the pan halfway through cooking.

7. Serve the French toast topped with the peaches along with a dollop of lightly sweetened whipped cream, coconut whipped topping, or vanilla yogurt.

DAIRY-FREE: Use vegan butter and serve with coconut whipped topping.

NUT-FREE: Use soy milk or nut-free milk instead of almond milk.

Bourbon Peaches

8 perfectly ripe peaches, peeled, pitted, and cut into wedges

3 tablespoons (45 mL) butter or vegan butter, divided

¼ cup + 2 tablespoons (90 mL) firmly packed brown sugar

6 tablespoons (90 mL) bourbon

2 teaspoons (10 mL) pure vanilla extract

Pinch of salt

French Toast

6 eggs

2 cups (500 mL) unsweetened almond milk

¼ cup (60 mL) pure maple syrup

1 teaspoon (5 mL) pure vanilla extract

½ teaspoon (2 mL) cinnamon

Pinch of salt

2 tablespoons (30 mL) butter or vegan butter, divided

2 tablespoons (30 mL) avocado oil or vegetable oil, divided

8 slices (each 1 inch/2.5 cm thick) white country loaf

Lightly sweetened whipped cream, coconut whipped topping, or vanilla yogurt, for serving

BREAKFAST ENCHILADAS

Serves 6

Packed with all the Mexican flavours that we love, these enchiladas take a bit of work but they are well worth it. You can make the Chipotle Sauce up to 5 days ahead and store it in the fridge until you are ready to pour it on the enchiladas before baking. For the record, we are pretty sure we are part Mexican and nobody has told us; we could eat Mexican food every single day! You can find chipotle peppers in adobo sauce in the Mexican food section of many grocery stores.

1. MAKE THE CHIPOTLE SAUCE In a medium saucepan, heat the olive oil over medium-low heat. Add the onions and cook for 5 to 8 minutes, until soft and translucent, stirring occasionally. Add the garlic cloves and cook until they start to soften, about 5 minutes, stirring to make sure you do not burn them.

2. Add the chopped tomatoes, chipotle peppers, sugar, salt, and water. Reduce the heat to low, cover, and cook for 30 to 40 minutes, stirring occasionally, until the tomatoes have completely broken down. If the sauce starts to get too thick, add a few more tablespoons of water.

3. Transfer the sauce to a deep bowl and blend with an immersion blender until smooth. Taste, and add more salt if needed. Set aside.

4. MAKE THE ENCHILADAS Preheat the oven to 375°F (190°C). Brush a 13- × 9-inch (3 L) baking dish with olive oil.

5. In a medium frying pan, heat the olive oil over medium-low heat. Add the onions and cook, stirring occasionally, until soft and translucent, 5 to 8 minutes. Add the sweet peppers and salt and cook until the peppers are slightly softened, 4 to 5 minutes. Remove from the heat.

6. In a large frying pan, melt the butter over low heat. Add the eggs and cook, frequently pulling, lifting, and folding the eggs until no liquid egg remains, about 4 minutes. Season with salt and black pepper to taste. Remove from the heat.

Chipotle Sauce

2 tablespoons (30 mL) extra-virgin olive oil

1 large sweet onion, finely chopped

2 cloves garlic, smashed

8 Roma tomatoes, chopped

2 chipotle peppers in adobo sauce

1 teaspoon (5 mL) sugar

½ teaspoon (2 mL) sea salt

½ cup (125 mL) water

Enchiladas

2 tablespoons (30 mL) extra-virgin olive oil

2 cups (500 mL) finely chopped yellow onion (1 large onion)

2 cups (500 mL) yellow, orange, and/or red sweet peppers cut into ½-inch (1 cm) pieces

¼ teaspoon (1 mL) salt

2 tablespoons (30 mL) butter or vegan butter

12 eggs, well beaten, or 1 batch Tofu Veggie Scramble (page 73)

Black pepper

6 large soft flour tortillas

Continued . . .

7. Working with one tortilla at a time, on the lower middle section of the tortilla, layer about ⅓ cup (75 mL) of scrambled eggs (or Tofu Veggie Scramble, if using), and a spoonful each of the beans, sweet pepper mixture, and the Chipotle Sauce. Wrap the tortilla starting at the end closest to you, tucking in the sides halfway through the roll. Transfer the roll to the prepared baking dish. Repeat with the remaining tortillas and fillings, arranging the tortillas so that they touch in the baking dish as shown. Spoon the remaining Chipotle Sauce evenly over the tortillas.

8. Bake until the sauce starts to bubble, about 45 minutes. Remove from the oven and sprinkle with the cilantro and avocado. Serve with lime wedges and sour cream (if using).

I cup (250 mL) drained and rinsed canned black beans

I cup (250 mL) chopped fresh cilantro

I avocado, pitted, peeled, and diced

For serving

Lime wedges

Sour cream or Vegan Sour Cream (page 315; optional)

VEGAN: Use vegan butter instead of butter and replace the eggs with Tofu Veggie Scramble (page 73).

GLUTEN-FREE: Use gluten-free tortillas.

NUT-FREE: Skip the Vegan Sour Cream.

WEST COAST EGGS BENNY

Serves 4

Living on the west coast of British Columbia has spoiled us a bit, especially when it comes to fish! Buy the best sustainably sourced smoked wild salmon you can find (you may have to do some homework to locate the best supplier in your area) and of course use the freshest free-range eggs possible: the fresher the eggs, the better they will hold together when poached. The no-fuss, foolproof hollandaise sauce was inspired by the Benny sauce that the Tomato Fresh Food Café in Vancouver used when Tori worked there years ago as a server to pay her way through university.

You will want to have everything prepared before you cook your eggs. We like to use vegan mayonnaise for the hollandaise, which may seem odd given that the dish isn't vegan, but it's a great example of a recipe where you can cut back a bit on animal products with zero taste compromise. It all counts!

1. Fill a large frying pan or very shallow pot three-quarters full with water and add the vinegar. Bring to a gentle simmer over medium heat.

2. MEANWHILE, MAKE THE HOLLANDAISE SAUCE Pour an inch of water into a small pot and bring to a simmer over medium heat.

3. In a small bowl, whisk together the mayonnaise, lemon juice, and mustard.

4. Place the butter in a glass bowl and set it over the simmering water (the bottom of the bowl should not touch the water). Once the butter is melted, whisk in the mayonnaise mixture until smooth. Add salt to taste. Remove from the heat but leave the bowl on top of the pot to stay warm.

5. MAKE THE EGGS BENNY Cut the English muffins in half and toast; butter the muffins if desired. Place a layer of smoked salmon on top of each toasted muffin half and place two halves on each plate.

6. Check that the frying pan of water is gently simmering. Crack one egg into a saucer or small bowl. Place the edge of the saucer as close to the simmering water as you can get (without burning yourself!) and gently slip the egg into the water. The egg whites will "feather" or spread out in

Eggs Benny

1 teaspoon (5 mL) white vinegar

4 English muffins

Butter or vegan butter (optional)

8 ounces (225 g) smoked wild salmon, thinly sliced

8 eggs

¼ cup (60 mL) chopped fresh dill

¼ cup (60 mL) finely chopped red onion or thinly sliced fresh chives

Salt and pepper

Hollandaise Sauce

½ cup (125 mL) mayonnaise or vegan mayonnaise

1 tablespoon (15 mL) fresh lemon juice

1 teaspoon (5 mL) Dijon mustard

3 tablespoons (45 mL) butter or vegan butter

Salt

Continued . . .

the pan; don't worry, and do not touch. Repeat with the remaining eggs (you may need to do this in two batches). After 2 minutes at a low simmer, gently ease a slotted spoon under each egg to loosen it from the bottom of the pan. Now the egg will float to the top. Cook for another 30 seconds to 2 minutes, depending how runny you want the yolks. Use the slotted spoon to lift each egg out of the water, then rest the spoon on a little stack of paper towel to wick away any water.

7. Place one poached egg on each prepared English muffin half. Spoon the warm Hollandaise Sauce over each egg and sprinkle with the fresh dill and red onion. Season with salt and pepper and serve immediately.

DAIRY-FREE: Use vegan butter.

GLUTEN-FREE: Use gluten-free bread instead of English muffins and use gluten-free mayonnaise.

TOFU VEGGIE SCRAMBLE

Serves 2 to 3

Scrambled tofu has a similar texture to traditional scrambled eggs. The chef at the Fairmont Kea Lani hotel, in Maui, taught Jillian how to make this scramble—it is very easy, and you'll be surprised how good it tastes! We love serving this with our fresh biscuits (see page 235 for a few variations), Crispy Roasted Rosemary Potatoes (page 210), a stack of Angel Cakes (page 63), or simply on a slice of toast. You can use whatever vegetables you have in your house, but we love this combo of mushrooms, tomatoes, and arugula or spinach. This makes an incredible substitute for the eggs in our Breakfast Enchiladas (page 67).

1. Press the tofu between 2 sheets of paper towel to remove excess moisture.

2. Heat 1 tablespoon (15 mL) of the vegan butter in a medium frying pan over medium heat. Add the onions and cook until soft and translucent, 3 to 4 minutes, stirring occasionally.

3. Add the mushrooms and garlic and cook, stirring occasionally, until the mushrooms are soft, 4 to 5 minutes. Transfer the vegetables to a small bowl.

4. Place the frying pan back on the stove over medium heat and add the remaining 1 tablespoon (15 mL) vegan butter. Once the pan is hot and the butter is melted, crumble the tofu into the pan with your fingers. Stir the tofu gently and cook until it is lightly browned, about 5 minutes.

5. Add the cooked vegetables, tomatoes, and spinach and stir until the greens are wilted. Remove from the heat and season with salt and pepper. Serve garnished with chives if desired.

1 package (12 ounces/350 g) medium-firm tofu, drained

2 tablespoons (30 mL) vegan butter, divided

½ cup (125 mL) finely chopped yellow onion

3 ounces (85 g) sliced white, brown, and/or shiitake mushrooms (about 1 cup/250 mL)

1 clove garlic, crushed

6 to 9 cherry tomatoes, halved or quartered

1 cup (250 mL) packed baby spinach or baby arugula

Salt and pepper

1 tablespoon (15 mL) sliced fresh chives, for garnish

BREAKFAST BRUSCHETTA

Serves 4

Bruschetta is commonly served topped with basil and tomatoes. A classic appetizer collides with breakfast in this fresh and flavour-packed dish. We often skip the eggs and instead whip up a batch of our Tofu Veggie Scramble (page 73).

1. Fill a large frying pan or very shallow pot three-quarters full with water. Bring to a gentle simmer over medium heat.

2. MEANWHILE, MAKE THE BASIL GUACAMOLE In a mini food processor, combine the basil, avocados, lime juice, and salt to taste. Process until smooth. Alternatively, finely chop the basil, then combine with the avocado, lime juice, and salt in a small bowl and mash with a fork until the avocado is smooth.

3. MAKE THE TOMATO BRUSCHETTA In a medium bowl, stir together the cherry tomatoes, basil, red onion, crushed garlic, olive oil, and salt.

4. Using a pastry brush, brush both sides of each baguette slice with olive oil and grill or broil the bread until lightly toasted. Rub one side of each piece with the cut side of the halved garlic clove and spread a heaping tablespoon of the Basil Guacamole on each toast.

5. POACH THE EGGS Crack one egg into a saucer or small bowl. Place the edge of the saucer as close to the simmering water as you can get (without burning yourself!) and gently slip the egg into the water. The egg whites will "feather" or spread out in the pan; don't worry and do not touch. Repeat with the remaining eggs (you may need to do this in two batches). After 2 minutes at a low simmer, gently ease a slotted spoon under each egg to loosen it from the bottom of the pan. Now the egg will float to the top. Cook for another 30 seconds to 2 minutes, depending how runny you want the yolks. Use the slotted spoon to lift each egg out of the water, then rest the spoon on a little stack of paper towel to wick away any water.

6. Top each toast with an egg, followed by a generous spoonful of the tomato mixture. Serve garnished with the extra basil.

VEGAN: Skip the eggs or make our Tofu Veggie Scramble (page 73) to replace the eggs.

GLUTEN-FREE: Use gluten-free bread instead of a baguette.

Basil Guacamole

½ cup (125 mL) loosely packed basil leaves

2 avocados, pitted, peeled, and chopped

Juice of 1 lime

Sea salt

Tomato Bruschetta

1½ cups (375 mL) sliced heirloom cherry tomatoes

⅓ cup (75 mL) chopped fresh basil leaves, more for garnish

2 tablespoons (30 mL) finely chopped red onion

1 clove garlic, crushed + 1 clove garlic, halved

1 tablespoon (15 mL) extra-virgin olive oil, more for the bread

½ teaspoon (2 mL) sea salt

8 thick, long diagonal slices of day-old baguette

8 eggs or 1 batch Tofu Veggie Scramble (page 73)

SWEETHEART OVEN FRIES

Serves 3 to 4

These sweet little fries will be the star of your Valentine's breakfast, lunch, or dinner! Serve them as hash browns to complement your eggs, as a side for your dinner, or just on their own as an adorable little snack. We love serving these fries with West Coast Eggs Benny (page 69), Breakfast Bruschetta (page 74), or Tofu Veggie Scramble (page 73). You will need a small heart-shaped cookie cutter to pull this one off.

6 large white or red potatoes

2 tablespoons (30 mL) olive oil

1 tablespoon (15 mL) chopped fresh rosemary

1 teaspoon (5 mL) sea salt

1. Preheat the oven to 450°F (230°C). Line a baking sheet with parchment paper.

2. Bring a large pot of salted water to a boil. Peel the potatoes (or just wash them—depends how you want to use the leftover potatoes after you cut them with the cookie cutter) and boil them for 15 minutes. Drain in a colander and let cool slightly.

3. Once cool enough to touch, cut the potatoes crosswise into ½-inch (1 cm) slices. Using a small heart-shaped cookie cutter, cut out as many hearts from each slice as you can.

4. Place the heart-shaped potatoes on the prepared baking sheet and toss with the olive oil, rosemary, and salt. Arrange in a single layer and bake until golden brown, about 30 minutes, carefully turning the potatoes with a metal spatula once halfway through the baking. Serve hot out of the oven on their own or with your favourite ketchup or dip.

PAUL'S BIRCHER MUESLI

Serves 4 to 6

One of the best things about growing our families has been the introduction of new dishes to the mix. When Jillian's fiancé Justin's parents joined our crew one Christmas, Paul whipped up his famous Bircher muesli, a Christmas tradition of their own. Paul's recipe came from the Westin Bayshore hotel in Vancouver, where he is a regular. After years of ordering muesli there, the chef finally gave in to Paul's charm and shared the recipe with him. We tweaked it a bit to give you a dairy-free option and added a hint of cinnamon. This truly is the original overnight oats—turns out the Swiss had it all figured out ages ago! The muesli will keep in the fridge for a few days, which makes it perfect for weekday breakfasts or a make-ahead breakfast for a crowd.

2 cups (500 mL) old-fashioned rolled oats

¾ cup (175 mL) unsweetened vanilla almond milk

2 cups (500 mL) finely chopped apples, plus extra slices for garnish (Ambrosia or Gala are good choices; peeling is optional)

¾ cup (175 mL) chopped raw almonds

¼ cup (60 mL) pure liquid honey or maple syrup

¼ cup (60 mL) table (18%) cream or Cashew Cream (page 313)

¼ teaspoon (1 mL) cinnamon, more for garnish

Pinch of sea salt

1. In a large bowl, combine the oats with the almond milk. Stir to combine, cover, and refrigerate for 4 to 6 hours or overnight.

2. Once the oats have soaked, add the apples, almonds, honey, cream, cinnamon, and salt. Stir to combine.

3. To serve, divide the muesli among small bowls, add a fresh slice of apple, and sprinkle with cinnamon.

VEGAN: Use Cashew Cream (page 313) instead of cream and maple syrup instead of honey.

GLUTEN-FREE: Use certified gluten-free rolled oats.

NUT-FREE: Skip the almonds or substitute hemp seeds. Use soy milk instead of almond milk and Cashew Cream.

BROILED GRAPEFRUIT
WITH COCONUT ALMOND GRANOLA

Serves 6

Food that looks as good as it tastes is a big deal in our world, and there is nothing prettier than a grapefruit! We both love grapefruit and agree that this is a sweet breakfast to serve for a Mother's Day brunch or just a casual weekend breakfast. The sweetness of the grapefruit is offset by the creamy yogurt, and the granola adds a perfect crunch. Tori has been making her own granola for years, and this coconut almond version is her best yet. If you can't find ribbon coconut, simply use the shredded variety.

1. **MAKE THE COCONUT ALMOND GRANOLA** Preheat the oven to 325°F (160°C). Line a baking sheet with parchment paper.

2. In a large bowl, combine the oats, ribbon coconut, flaked coconut, sliced almonds, chopped almonds, hemp seeds, cinnamon, and salt; stir well.

3. In a small bowl, stir together the coconut oil, maple syrup, vanilla, and almond extract.

4. Slowly add the coconut oil mixture to the oat mixture while stirring to combine.

5. Evenly spread the mixture on the prepared baking sheet. Bake until light golden brown, stirring every 10 minutes, for about 20 minutes in total. Cool before serving. Store granola in an airtight container for up to 1 month.

6. **MAKE THE BROILED GRAPEFRUIT** Position an oven rack so that your grapefruit will be close to the broiler but not touching and preheat the broiler. Line a baking sheet with parchment paper.

7. Run a grapefruit knife or sharp paring knife first around the perimeter of each grapefruit half to separate the flesh from the pith (the bitter white part), then along the edge of each segment to loosen it from the membranes. Place the grapefruit halves cut side up on the prepared baking sheet.

8. In a small bowl, stir together the maple syrup, melted butter, and cinnamon. Spoon a couple of teaspoons of the maple syrup mixture over each grapefruit half, gently spreading it with the back of the spoon to evenly coat each half.

Coconut Almond Granola

2 cups (500 mL) old-fashioned rolled oats

1 cup (250 mL) unsweetened ribbon coconut

1 cup (250 mL) sweetened flaked coconut

1 cup (250 mL) sliced raw almonds

½ cup (125 mL) roughly chopped whole raw almonds

½ cup (125 mL) hemp seeds

½ teaspoon (2 mL) cinnamon

Generous pinch of sea salt

⅔ cup (150 mL) coconut oil, melted

⅓ cup (75 mL) pure maple syrup

1 teaspoon (5 mL) pure vanilla extract

1 teaspoon (5 mL) pure almond extract

Broiled Grapefruit

3 large pink grapefruits, cut in half crosswise

¼ cup (60 mL) pure maple syrup

2 tablespoons (30 mL) butter or vegan butter, melted

1 teaspoon (5 mL) cinnamon

Vanilla Greek yogurt or dairy-free vanilla yogurt, for serving

Continued . . .

9. Broil for 5 to 7 minutes, until the grapefruit just starts to caramelize. To serve, place the grapefruit halves on plates and top with a spoonful of yogurt and some Coconut Almond Granola.

VEGAN: Use vegan butter and your favourite non-dairy yogurt.

GLUTEN-FREE: Use certified gluten-free rolled oats and coconut.

NUT-FREE: Replace the sliced almonds with 1 cup (250 mL) of rolled oats and replace the whole almonds with 1 cup (250 mL) of unsweetened shredded coconut. Skip the almond extract.

VANILLA CHERRY SCONES

Makes 8 scones

We created these scones at the height of cherry season when they were as ripe and perfect as Mother Nature makes them in the Okanagan. These scones are drop-dead gorgeous and are so perfect to make for a brunch or really any occasion during cherry season. The secret to a tender scone is to not overmix the dough and to keep the butter as cold as you can. These received rave reviews during testing and disappeared in minutes, so you may want to consider making a double batch. Just saying.

1. Preheat the oven to 450°F (230°C). Line a baking sheet with parchment paper.

2. In a small liquid measuring cup, whisk the egg. Add almond milk to the ¾-cup (175 mL) mark. Whisk in the vanilla.

3. In a large bowl, combine the flour, sugar, baking powder, and salt; whisk to combine. Add the butter and, using your fingers or a pastry blender, break up the butter until the pieces are the size of peas.

4. Add the milk mixture and the cherries to the flour mixture and gently mix together with a rubber spatula in a turning motion until just combined (do not overmix!). The dough will look rough and uneven. Empty the dough onto a lightly floured work surface. Pat and gently shape the dough until it sticks together in a disc about 1½ inches (4 cm) thick. Transfer to the prepared baking sheet.

5. Using a sharp knife, cut the disc into 8 pie-shaped pieces and separate the scones slightly. If desired, using a pastry brush, brush each scone with cream or almond milk and sprinkle lightly with coarse sugar. Bake until golden brown, 15 to 20 minutes. Serve warm.

VEGAN: Omit the egg and use a full ¾ cup (175 mL) almond milk. Use almond milk instead of cream and use vegan butter.

NUT-FREE: Use soy milk or other nut-free milk instead of almond milk.

I egg, at room temperature

½ to ¾ cup (125 to 175 mL) unsweetened almond milk

I teaspoon (5 mL) pure vanilla extract

2 cups (500 mL) all-purpose flour

¼ cup (60 mL) sugar

4 teaspoons (20 mL) baking powder

¼ teaspoon (I mL) salt

⅓ cup (75 mL) cold butter or vegan butter

I cup (250 mL) fresh cherries, pitted and cut into quarters (see Tip)

2 tablespoons (30 mL) table (18%) cream or unsweetened almond milk (optional)

2 tablespoons (30 mL) coarse sugar (optional)

TIP: You can substitute frozen pitted cherries for fresh cherries in the off-season. Cut them in quarters while frozen and do not thaw before mixing them in.

a

b

c

d

SUNSHINE MUFFINS

Makes 24 muffins

Everyone has a go-to muffin recipe, and this is Tori's. They were born out of a moment of frustration when her kids were not eating their veggies. (A dietitian's kids can be picky too!) These muffins are packed with fruits and veggies, including beets. The batter looks pink when you mix it, but it disappears when you bake them. A food processor with a shredding blade will be your best friend here. This recipe makes a lot of muffins, but they freeze beautifully in a resealable bag for quick snacks or breakfasts on the go. Skip the nuts if you want them to be kid-lunch-friendly, of course. If you're wondering what the kids thought, Charlie gave them a 20 out of 10. We'll take it!

1. Position racks in the top and bottom thirds of the oven and preheat the oven to 350°F (180°C). Grease 2 muffin tins or line with paper liners.

2. In a large bowl, stir together the apple, carrots, beets, zucchini, eggs, olive oil, and vanilla.

3. In a medium bowl, sift together the all-purpose flour, whole wheat flour, sugar, baking powder, baking soda, salt, cinnamon, allspice, and nutmeg.

4. Stir the flour mixture into the vegetable mixture until well combined. Fold in the raisins and chopped nuts (if using).

5. Fill the muffin cups about three-quarters full. Top each muffin with a pecan half (if using). Bake for 20 to 25 minutes, or until golden brown and a toothpick inserted into the centre of a muffin comes out clean, rotating the muffin tins top to bottom and front to back halfway through. Let cool completely in the muffin tins on a rack before removing from the tins. Store in a resealable container at room temperature for a few days or in the freezer for up to 1 month.

VEGAN: Replace the eggs with Flax or Chia Eggs (page 315); the muffins turn out denser but equally delicious.

NUT-FREE: Skip the nuts.

2 cups (500 mL) grated peeled apple (2 to 3 large Spartan, Gala, or McIntosh)

1½ cups (375 mL) grated peeled carrots (2 to 3 medium carrots)

1½ cups (375 mL) grated peeled red beets (2 to 3 medium beets)

1 cup (250 mL) grated zucchini (1 small zucchini)

6 eggs, well beaten, or Flax or Chia Eggs (page 315; see below)

1½ cups (375 mL) extra-virgin olive oil, avocado oil, or vegetable oil

2 teaspoons (10 mL) pure vanilla extract

2 cups (500 mL) all-purpose flour

2½ cups (625 mL) whole wheat flour

1½ cups (375 mL) sugar or coconut sugar

4 teaspoons (20 mL) baking powder

2 teaspoons (10 mL) baking soda

1 teaspoon (5 mL) salt

1 tablespoon (15 mL) cinnamon

1 teaspoon (5 mL) ground allspice

¼ teaspoon (1 mL) nutmeg

2 cups (500 mL) raisins

1 cup (250 mL) chopped toasted raw walnuts or pecans (optional)

24 raw pecan halves, for topping (optional)

UKRAINIAN CHRISTMAS WHEAT (KUTIA)
WITH POPPY SEED PASTE

Serves 10 to 12

This rustic and hearty sweet porridge-like dish is the first of twelve courses in a traditional Ukrainian Christmas Eve supper; the wheat represents the staff of life. Since we are a bunch of rebels, we have had it as our Christmas breakfast for as long as we can remember. This dish is super healthy, and though we serve it for Christmas it would make a great alternative to oatmeal any day of the year! We do not always make the poppy seed paste; some of us love our kutia topped simply with brown sugar, a sprinkle of cinnamon, and our favourite milk.

Note that 2 cups (500 mL) of uncooked wheat berries is enough to serve 8 to 10 people, if you want to reduce the recipe a bit.

1. PREPARE THE WHEAT BERRIES Preheat the oven to 350°F (180°C).

2. Rinse the wheat berries in a sieve and spread them evenly on a baking sheet. (You can line it with parchment paper to make the wheat easier to transfer off the baking sheet, though it's not necessary.) Roast the wheat berries for 10 minutes. Stir them on the baking sheet, and continue roasting until the wheat smells nutty, about 10 minutes more. Remove from the oven and let cool.

3. Transfer the wheat berries to a large pot and add enough water to cover it by 2 inches (5 cm). Simmer, uncovered and stirring occasionally, until the wheat berries start to split and are soft but still bouncy to the bite, 2 to 3 hours. You may need to add more water as it cooks, keeping it to the level of the wheat until near the end of the cooking time. There should be little or no water left at the end of the cooking.

4. MEANWHILE, MAKE THE POPPY SEED PASTE In a small bowl, cover the raisins with boiling water and let soak for 20 minutes. Drain the raisins and transfer to a small food processor.

5. In a coffee or spice grinder, pulse the poppy seeds a few times just until they stick together. Add them to the food processor along with the honey, melted butter, and salt. Process until the mixture forms a smooth paste, about 1 minute.

6. To serve, divide the warmed wheat among bowls. Top with a generous scoop of the Poppy Seed Paste and cream or your favourite non-dairy milk, and stir.

3 cups (750 mL) spring wheat berries

Poppy Seed Paste

2 tablespoons (30 mL) raisins

½ cup (125 mL) poppy seeds

1 tablespoon (15 mL) pure creamed honey or maple syrup

1 tablespoon (15 mL) butter or vegan butter, melted

Pinch of salt

Table (18%) cream or your favourite non-dairy milk, for serving

VEGAN: Substitute maple syrup for the honey and use vegan butter in the Poppy Seed Paste. Use a non-dairy milk (soy milk or other nut-free milk, if required) for serving.

APPETIZERS & SNACKS

SWEET AND SPICY NUTS

Makes 1½ cups (375 mL)

These showy nuts are deceptively easy to make. In fact, you can whip them up in under 3 minutes and still look like Martha Stewart. Serve these as a snack or on top of a salad with goat cheese, or put them in little bags tied with a ribbon for adorable hostess gifts. Trust us, these nuts do not last long! You might want to make a double or triple batch (using a larger frying pan). You can use most any type of nut that you like in this recipe. Reduce the cayenne pepper by half if you do not like too much spice.

1. Lay a 24-inch (60 cm) length of parchment paper on a work surface.

2. In a medium frying pan, heat the vegan butter and maple syrup over medium-low heat until the mixture bubbles. Cook for 1 minute, stirring with a wooden spoon, being careful to not burn the mixture.

3. Add the almonds, cashews, pecans, salt, and cayenne pepper and cook, stirring, for an additional 2 to 3 minutes (use a timer). The nuts will appear sticky and the coating will look slightly thickened and caramelized.

4. Immediately empty the nuts out onto the parchment paper, spreading them out with your wooden spoon, and let cool completely before serving. These are best served the same day, but can be stored in an airtight container at room temperature for up to 1 week.

1 tablespoon (15 mL) vegan butter

¼ cup (60 mL) pure maple syrup

½ cup (125 mL) whole raw almonds

½ cup (125 mL) roasted raw cashews

½ cup (125 mL) raw pecan halves

¼ teaspoon (1 mL) sea salt

¼ teaspoon (1 mL) cayenne pepper

GREEN GARLIC BREAD

Serves 6 to 8

We love our greens. We also love garlic bread. So, green garlic bread, anyone? We guarantee this will not disappoint. This bread has a crusty exterior and a soft herby garlicky interior, and it's easily made vegan (see below). Serve this at your next barbecue alongside Summer Herbed Grilled Vegetables (page 224) or as a side for Garden Bolognese (page 158) or Captain's Kale Caesar Salad (page 131) for an impressive crowd-pleaser.

1. Preheat the oven to 400°F (200°C). Line a baking sheet with parchment paper.

2. Using a bread knife, cut the loaf of bread into 1-inch (2.5 cm) thick slices without cutting all the way through, stopping just short of the bottom so the loaf stays intact. Place the loaf on the prepared baking sheet.

3. In a mini food processor or blender with a narrow bottom, combine the melted butter, olive oil, basil, parsley, chives, salt, and garlic. Blend until smooth.

4. Using a large pastry brush, apply enough of the butter mixture to coat both sides of each slice of bread, gently pulling the slices apart and working your way along the loaf until each slice is coated.

5. Place the sprigs of rosemary between slices, spacing them evenly along the loaf and leaving the ends of the rosemary sticking out. Sprinkle the loaf with the cheese (if using). Bake until the bread is hot throughout and the loaf is crusty and light brown on top, 10 to 15 minutes. Serve immediately.

VEGAN: Use vegan butter and skip the cheese.

1 day-old loaf crusty white country loaf or ciabatta

½ cup (125 mL) butter or vegan butter, melted

2 tablespoons (30 mL) extra-virgin olive oil

½ cup (125 mL) loosely packed fresh basil leaves

½ cup (125 mL) loosely packed fresh flat-leaf parsley leaves

¼ cup (60 mL) sliced fresh chives

½ teaspoon (2 mL) sea salt

3 large cloves garlic

3 sprigs fresh rosemary

½ cup (125 mL) grated Asiago or Parmesan cheese (optional)

MUSHROOM KALE GARLIC TOASTS

Serves 8 to 10

Garlicky mushrooms and kale come together like long lost soul mates to create a healthier but equally decadent tasting crostini topping for your next round of guests. These are super easy to whip up in a flash and the earthy, simple flavours make these a total crowd-pleaser, especially for those cozy fall or winter evenings when the wine is flowing and the fire is crackling. Pass the merlot!

1. Preheat the broiler. Line a baking sheet with parchment paper.

2. Place the baguette slices on the baking sheet and brush both sides with olive oil. Broil until golden brown on one side. Flip the slices and broil until the other side is golden brown. Remove from the oven and rub one side of the baguette slices with the halved clove of garlic. Lightly spread goat cheese on each slice. Set aside.

3. In a large frying pan, heat the olive oil and butter over medium heat. Add the crushed garlic and cook, stirring, until translucent, about 30 seconds. Add the mushrooms and cook, stirring frequently, until they are soft, about 5 minutes. Stir in the kale and continue to cook until the kale is wilted but still bright green, about 3 minutes. Remove from the heat and season with salt and pepper.

4. To serve, place the baguette slices on a platter, spoon 1 tablespoon (15 mL) of the mushroom and kale mixture on each slice, and sprinkle with the chives.

VEGAN: Use spreadable herb cashew cheese instead of goat cheese and use vegan butter.

8 to 10 slices (½ inch/1 cm each) day-old baguette

2 tablespoons (30 mL) extra-virgin olive oil, more for brushing the baguette

1 clove garlic, halved + 2 cloves garlic, crushed

½ cup (125 mL) herb goat cheese or spreadable herb cashew cheese

1 tablespoon (15 mL) butter or vegan butter

12 ounces (340 g) sliced white or brown mushrooms (about 4 cups/1 L)

3 cups (750 mL) loosely packed green curly kale, stems removed, torn into bite-size pieces

Salt and pepper

3 tablespoons (45 mL) thinly sliced fresh chives

SUMMER SQUASH HERB TART

Serves 12 to 14

When gardens and markets are overflowing with gorgeous zucchini, we highly recommend making this tart. We are big fans of spending less time slaving in the kitchen on those hot summer days! This tart uses time-saving puff pastry as a base (nothing fancy required), and gorgeous ribbons of zucchini dress it up, making it a rustic but impressive appetizer or light lunch. Frozen puff pastry is a cook's best friend. We always have a few packages in our freezers.

1. Preheat the oven to 425°F (220°C). Have a baking sheet on hand.

2. Place a large piece of parchment paper (about 12 × 20 inches/30 × 50 cm) on a work surface, roll out the puff pastry into a 10 x 15-inch (25 × 38 cm) rectangle. It doesn't have to be exact. Using the over-hanging parchment as handles, holding it taut, carefully transfer the parchment and pastry to the baking sheet.

3. In a medium bowl, combine the cheese, cream, 1 tablespoon (15 mL) of the chives, thyme, ½ teaspoon (2 mL) of the salt, and 1 clove of the crushed garlic. Mix well. Spread evenly over the puff pastry, leaving a ¼-inch (5 mm) edge uncovered.

4. In a large bowl, toss the zucchini ribbons with the olive oil, remaining ½ teaspoon (2 mL) salt, pepper, and remaining 1 clove crushed garlic. Layer the zucchini ribbons over the cheese filling in a twisting fashion; the ribbons will overlap slightly.

5. Bake until the edges are puffed and golden brown, 20 to 25 minutes. Sprinkle with the remaining 1 tablespoon (15 mL) chives. Slide the tart onto a cutting board and cut into squares. Garnish with thyme sprigs and serve.

VEGAN: Use vegan puff pastry. Use Cashew Cream (page 313) instead of cream and use a spreadable herb cashew cheese instead of goat cheese or skip the cheese layer.

---

1 sheet puff pastry, thawed (from a block of puff pastry)

½ cup (125 mL) soft goat cheese or spreadable herb cashew cheese (5½ ounces/150 g)

2 to 3 tablespoons (30 to 45 mL) 10% cream or Cashew Cream (page 313)

2 tablespoons (30 mL) sliced fresh chives, divided

1 tablespoon (15 mL) fresh thyme leaves

1 teaspoon (5 mL) salt, divided

2 cloves garlic, crushed, divided

3 cups (750 mL) zucchini ribbons, shaved with a vegetable peeler (2 small zucchini; mix of green and yellow)

1 tablespoon (15 mL) olive oil

½ teaspoon (2 mL) pepper

2 or 3 sprigs fresh thyme

SWEET CHILI TOFU

Serves 6 to 8

Sweet chili chicken is one of our all-time favourite appetizers at Vancouver's Cactus Club Cafe (we are regulars and Jillian used to work there). Of course we had to give it a facelift to make it plant-based, and bam, we nailed it! This is a dead-ringer for the real deal. It's super crispy with a flavourful tofu interior and coated in a perfect amount of sweet and spicy sauce that you will be addicted to, guaranteed! Pressing the tofu and then soaking it in vegetable stock allows it to soak up more flavour when cooked, but you can skip this step if you forget or do not have time. Be warned, the glaze is very thick! (We are thrilled that Cactus Club now has a vegan tofu version on their menu.)

1. PREPARE THE TOFU Press the tofu by placing it between 2 sheets of paper towel, then sandwich it between 2 plates. Place a heavy object such as a stack of books on top; let sit for 1 hour. Cut the tofu into 1-inch (2.5 cm) cubes and gently press with a kitchen towel or paper towel to remove any remaining liquid.

2. Place the tofu in a small, shallow bowl or plastic container, then pour the stock over it to cover. Cover with a lid or plastic wrap and refrigerate for at least 4 hours or overnight.

3. MAKE THE SRIRACHA MAYONNAISE Stir together the vegan mayonnaise and the Sriracha in a small bowl. Set aside.

4. Set out 3 shallow bowls. Place the almond milk in one bowl. In the second bowl, stir together the cornstarch, ½ teaspoon (2 mL) salt, ½ teaspoon (2 mL) garlic powder, and ½ teaspoon (2 mL) paprika. In the third bowl, stir together the panko crumbs, the remaining ½ teaspoon (2 mL) salt, remaining ½ teaspoon (2 mL) garlic powder, and remaining ½ teaspoon (2 mL) paprika.

Tofu

1 package (12 ounces/350 g) extra-firm tofu, drained

1 cup (250 mL) chicken-flavoured vegetarian stock or vegetable stock

1 cup (250 mL) unsweetened almond milk

¾ cup (175 mL) cornstarch

1 teaspoon (5 mL) salt, divided

1 teaspoon (5 mL) garlic powder, divided

1 teaspoon (5 mL) sweet paprika, divided

1 cup (250 mL) panko crumbs

¼ to ½ cup (60 to 125 mL) avocado oil or grapeseed oil

2 tablespoons (30 mL) sesame seeds

½ cup (125 mL) chopped fresh cilantro

3 green onions (white and light green parts only), sliced

Sriracha Mayonnaise

½ cup (125 mL) vegan mayonnaise

2 teaspoons (10 mL) Sriracha

Continued . . .

Sweet Chili Tofu continued

5. MAKE THE SWEET CHILI GLAZE Heat the avocado oil in a small saucepan over medium heat. Add the ginger and garlic and cook until fragrant, about 2 minutes, stirring frequently. Stir in the Thai chili sauce and rice wine vinegar.

6. Stir together the cornstarch and water in a small glass until smooth. Add the cornstarch mixture to the sauce and cook on a low boil, stirring, until it is thickened and clear, 1 to 2 minutes. Remove from the heat and set aside.

7. To prepare the tofu, place half of the tofu cubes in the seasoned cornstarch and toss to coat. Remove them from the cornstarch and place them in the almond milk, turning to coat. Finish with the panko coating, lightly pressing it in on all sides.

8. Heat ¼ cup (60 mL) avocado oil in a medium frying pan over medium heat. Working in batches so as not to crowd the pan, cook the tofu until golden brown on all sides, 4 to 5 minutes. Transfer the tofu to a medium bowl. Repeat with the remaining tofu, adding more oil if needed. Once all the tofu is cooked, pour a small amount of the Sweet Chili Glaze over the tofu cubes and gently toss to coat using a pair of tongs. Add as much Sweet Chili Glaze as desired—you will likely not use it all.

9. Arrange the tofu on a small platter, sprinkle with the sesame seeds, cilantro, and green onion, and serve immediately with the Sriracha Mayonnaise on the side.

***

GLUTEN-FREE: Use gluten-free vegetable stock.

NUT-FREE: Use soy milk or any nut-free milk instead of almond milk.

Sweet Chili Glaze

2 tablespoons (30 mL) avocado oil or grapeseed oil

2 teaspoons (10 mL) grated fresh ginger

2 cloves garlic, crushed

½ cup (125 mL) Thai sweet chili sauce

1 teaspoon (5 mL) rice wine vinegar

1 teaspoon (5 mL) cornstarch

2 tablespoons (30 mL) water

RAINBOW SALAD ROLLS WITH CRISPY TOFU

Makes 12 rolls; serves 6

Salad rolls are the epitome of summer food. Cram as many fresh veggies as you can into these! We give you some of our favourite filling suggestions, but do not stop there: try sliced kiwi fruit, or radishes or play around with the herbs such as basil or mint—the sky is the limit. These salad rolls take some time to prepare, but they are well worth the effort.

1. PREPARE THE CRISPY TOFU Press the tofu between layers of paper towel or a kitchen towel to remove extra moisture. Cut the tofu into 3-× ½-inch (8 × 1 cm) slices (they do not have to be exact) and place in a medium, shallow dish.

2. In a small saucepan, combine the ginger, garlic, soy sauce, black rice vinegar, brown sugar, and sesame oil. Bring to a simmer over medium heat and simmer for 1 minute, stirring to dissolve the sugar. Pour the mixture over the tofu, gently turn the slices to coat all of the tofu, and let marinate at room temperature for 1 hour.

3. MEANWHILE, MAKE THE PEANUT DIPPING SAUCE In a medium bowl, combine the peanut butter, water, lime juice, soy sauce, brown sugar, and garlic; whisk until smooth. Alternatively, combine ingredients in a blender or mini food processor and blend until smooth. Set aside.

4. COOK THE CRISPY TOFU Remove the tofu from the marinade. Pour the marinade into a small saucepan and bring to a simmer over medium-low heat. Simmer until slightly reduced, about 3 minutes. Strain to remove the ginger and set aside.

5. In a large frying pan, heat 1 tablespoon (15 mL) sesame oil and 1 tablespoon (15 mL) olive oil over medium heat. Cook the tofu (in batches so you don't crowd the pan), turning once, until golden brown on each side, about 2 minutes a side. Transfer to a plate. Repeat until all the tofu is cooked, adding more sesame oil and olive oil if needed.

Crispy Tofu

2 packages (12 ounces/350 g each) extra-firm tofu, drained

3-inch (8 cm) piece fresh ginger, peeled and thinly sliced

2 cloves garlic, thinly sliced

⅓ cup (75 mL) soy sauce

¼ cup (60 mL) black rice vinegar

3 tablespoons (45 mL) brown sugar

1 tablespoon (15 mL) sesame oil

Sesame oil and extra-virgin olive oil, for cooking

Peanut Dipping Sauce

½ cup (125 mL) creamy natural peanut butter

¼ cup (60 mL) warm water

Juice of 1 lime

2 tablespoons (30 mL) soy sauce

1 tablespoon (15 mL) firmly packed brown sugar

1 clove garlic, crushed

Continued . . .

6. ASSEMBLE THE SALAD ROLLS Bring a large pot of water to a boil. Add the rice vermicelli and cook until tender. Drain, rinse under cold water, and place in a small bowl.

7. Fill a shallow dish large enough to accommodate the rice-paper wrappers (such as a large pie plate) with warm water. Submerge one of the wrappers in the warm water until softened but still slightly stiff, 15 to 25 seconds. (If you wait until it is entirely softened, it is more likely to tear when you assemble the rolls.) Lay the softened wrapper on a clean work surface. In the lower-middle of each wrapper, layer a slice of avocado, some vermicelli noodles, your choice of vegetables, a few cilantro leaves, a slice of Crispy Tofu, and a sprinkle of peanuts. Fold the sides of the wrapper over the filling, then roll it up, starting from the bottom. Repeat filling and rolling the remaining salad rolls.

8. Serve with the Peanut Dipping Sauce, Sriracha, and hoisin sauce (if using) on the side.

GLUTEN-FREE: Use gluten-free soy sauce, vinegar, and hoisin sauce.

NUT-FREE: Skip the Peanut Dipping Sauce and use additional hoisin or Sriracha sauce as a dipping sauce.

Salad Rolls

9 ounces (250 g) dried rice vermicelli noodles

12 (9-inch/23 cm) rice-paper wrappers

1 ripe avocado, pitted, peeled, and thinly sliced

Leaves from 1 bunch fresh cilantro

½ cup (125 mL) roughly chopped unsalted peanuts

Vegetable filling suggestions (use as many as you like)

1 cup (250 mL) grated carrot or long, thin ribbons

1 candy cane beet, thinly sliced on a mandoline

½ English cucumber, thinly sliced into long ribbons

3 green onions (white and light green parts only), thinly sliced into long ribbons

1 mango, peeled and thinly sliced

1 red sweet pepper, thinly sliced

1 cup (250 mL) sugar peas (about 24 peas)

1 cup (250 mL) pea shoots

1 cup (250 mL) shaved red cabbage

For serving (optional)

Sriracha

Hoisin sauce

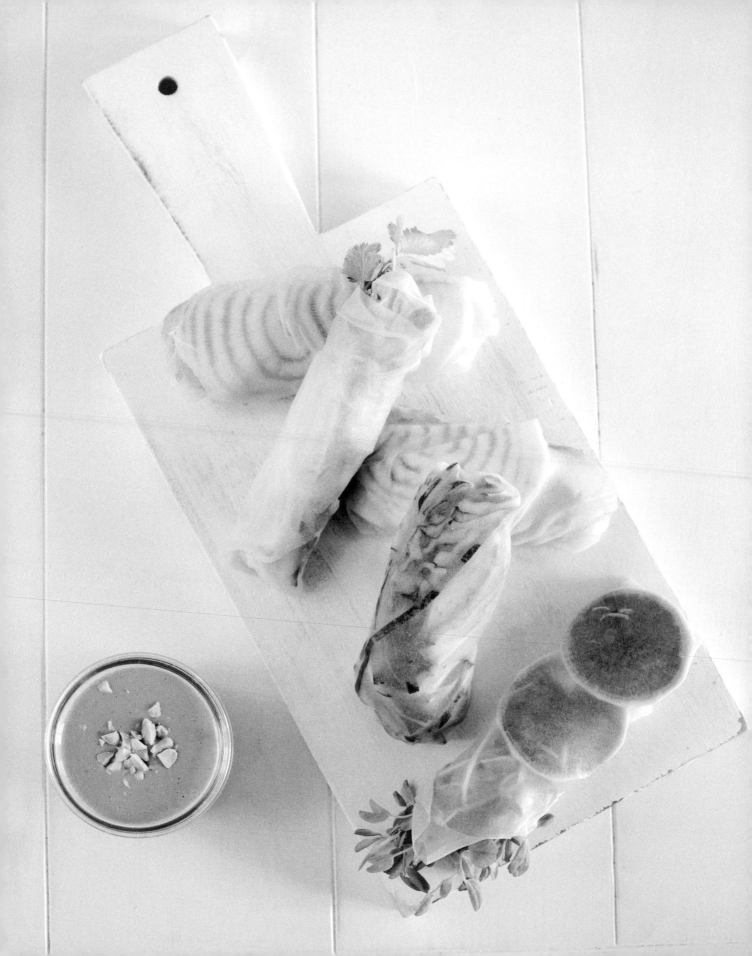

SUSHI POCKETS

Makes 12 to 15 pockets

This is such an impressive appetizer and far simpler to assemble than it looks! Inari (sushi pockets) is a traditional Japanese dish usually served with just the rice and the tofu pocket. Of course, we love the idea of filling them to the brim with anything our heart desires. We've included suggestions, but feel free to put your own spin on them. Do not be tempted to skip washing the rice: this step removes excess surface starch that can otherwise make the rice too sticky and starchy. You can find tofu pockets in the refrigerated section at any Asian food store—they are such a cool invention!

1. Place the rice in a sieve and rinse under cool running water until the water runs clear. Tip the rice out onto a large plate and set aside to dry for 30 minutes.

2. Add the rice along with the water to a medium pot and bring to a simmer. Cover and cook at a medium simmer for 10 minutes. Reduce the heat to low and cook for an additional 10 minutes, or until the rice is tender and the water is absorbed. Remove from the heat and let the rice sit, covered, for 15 minutes.

3. Meanwhile, in a small bowl, stir together the rice wine vinegar, sugar, and salt.

4. Once the rice is done, slowly add the vinegar mixture, gently stirring by cutting through the rice with a rice paddle or rubber spatula.

5. Place a bowl of room-temperature water beside the rice and the tofu pockets. Using wet fingers, press the rice into balls that will fit inside the tofu pockets, leaving some room for the other fillings.

6. Arrange the tofu pockets on a platter and sprinkle with the sesame seeds. Arrange the other fillings in bowls and let guests stuff their tofu pockets with whatever ingredients they like.

2 cups (500 mL) sushi rice

2 cups (500 mL) water

¼ cup (60 mL) rice wine vinegar

3 tablespoons (45 mL) sugar

1 teaspoon (5 mL) salt

12 to 15 inari tofu pockets

Black sesame seeds

Filling suggestions

English cucumber, sliced about ⅛ inch (3 mm) thick

Mango, peeled and sliced about ⅛ inch (3 mm) thick

Carrot, peeled and grated

Pea shoots

Smoked wild salmon, sliced about ⅛ inch (3 mm) thick

Wasabi

Pickled ginger

Soy sauce

VEGAN: Skip the salmon.

CREAMY SPINACH AND ARTICHOKE DIP

Serves 10 to 12

Many people know Shay (a friend and member of Team Jilly) for her impeccable taste and style, but this girl can also cook! Shay made this dip for a party Jillian hosted, and it disappeared in minutes. A traditional spinach and artichoke dip is made with loads of cheese, but you really don't miss it in this vegan version thanks to the creaminess of the cashews and the nutritional yeast that gives it a cheesy flavour. If you have never made something with these plant-based ingredients, this is a great recipe to get your feet wet! You will want to use a high-speed blender to get the best results. You will need to soak the cashews overnight (up to 12 hours) before starting this recipe.

1. Soak the cashews in water for at least 4 hours or overnight (up to 12 hours) in the fridge. Drain and rinse before using (see Tip).

2. In a high-speed blender, blend together the drained cashews, tofu, nutritional yeast, water, and cider vinegar until smooth. Set aside.

3. In a medium cast-iron frying pan, heat the olive oil over medium-low heat. Add the onions and cook until they are soft and translucent, 5 to 8 minutes, stirring occasionally. Reduce the heat to low and cook for an additional 20 minutes to slightly caramelize the onions, stirring occasionally.

4. Increase the heat to medium-low and add the crushed garlic. Cook until the garlic is fragrant, 30 to 60 seconds. Add the spinach, artichoke hearts, lemon juice, Greek seasoning, chili flakes, the tofu mixture, and salt to taste. Cook, stirring, until the dip is hot and everything is well incorporated. Add more water to thin the dip to a desired consistency, if needed.

5. Scrape the dip into a serving bowl and serve warm with tortilla chips, toasted pita bread, or cut-up raw vegetables.

GLUTEN-FREE: Serve with gluten-free tortilla chips or gluten-free pita.

2 cups (500 mL) raw cashews

1 package (12 ounces/350 g) medium-firm tofu, drained

½ cup (125 mL) nutritional yeast

¾ cup (175 mL) water, more if needed

2 teaspoons (10 mL) apple cider vinegar

2 tablespoons (30 mL) extra-virgin olive oil

2 cups (500 mL) finely chopped yellow onion (1 large onion)

2 cloves garlic, crushed

1 package (10½ ounces/300 g) frozen spinach, thawed and well drained

1 cup (250 mL) finely chopped marinated artichoke hearts

2 tablespoons + 1½ teaspoons (37 mL) fresh lemon juice

1 teaspoon (5 mL) Greek seasoning

¼ teaspoon (1 mL) red chili flakes

Sea salt

Tortilla chips, toasted pita bread, or cut-up raw vegetables, for serving

---

TIP: The overnight soak works best, but if you don't have time to soak the cashews for several hours (or forgot), you can use the quick method: soak them in boiling water for 30 minutes, then drain and rinse.

ROSEMARY POLENTA FRIES
WITH SMOKY TOMATO DIP

Serves 8

Humdrum ol' polenta (sorry, polenta, but it's true, you're just not that exciting on your own) gets an overhaul in these irresistibly crunchy rosemary "fries" with a soft interior. All our favourite flavours showed up for this dish! You can do most of the prep ahead of time, which puts these fries high on our go-to list for entertaining. You can use regular canned tomatoes if you don't have fire-roasted ones on hand—both work well.

1. MAKE THE ROSEMARY POLENTA FRIES Line an 8-inch (2 L) square baking dish with plastic wrap.

2. In a medium saucepan, bring the vegetable stock to a low boil. Slowly add the cornmeal while stirring and cook, stirring, until it is very thick, about 5 minutes. Stir in the Parmesan along with the butter.

3. Scrape the polenta into the prepared baking dish. Using a moistened rubber spatula, evenly press the polenta down into the dish. Cover with plastic wrap and refrigerate until chilled, at least 2 hours.

4. MEANWHILE, MAKE THE SMOKY TOMATO DIP Heat the olive oil in a medium saucepan over medium-low heat. Add the onions and cook until soft and translucent, 5 to 8 minutes, stirring occasionally. Add the garlic and cook for 1 minute, stirring occasionally.

5. Stir in the tomatoes with their liquid, basil, oregano, and sugar. Simmer for 10 minutes, stirring occasionally.

6. Purée the tomato sauce with an immersion blender or in a blender until it is smooth; you may need to add a bit of water to thin it. Season with salt and set aside.

7. FINISH THE FRIES Reheat the Smoky Tomato Dip and keep warm. Turn the polenta out onto a cutting board and cut into ½- × 2-inch (1 × 5 cm) fries.

Rosemary Polenta Fries

4 cups (1 L) vegetable stock

1½ cups (375 mL) yellow cornmeal

½ cup (125 mL) grated Parmesan cheese or Vegan Parm (page 314)

1 tablespoon (15 mL) butter or vegan butter

¼ to ½ cup (60 to 125 mL) extra-virgin olive oil

3 tablespoons (45 mL) chopped fresh rosemary

Sea salt or fleur de sel

2 or 3 sprigs fresh rosemary, for garnish

Smoky Tomato Dip

2 tablespoons (30 mL) extra-virgin olive oil

1 cup (250 mL) finely chopped sweet onion

2 cloves garlic, crushed

1 can (14 ounces/398 mL) fire-roasted tomatoes

½ cup (125 mL) chopped fresh basil

1 teaspoon (5 mL) dried oregano

1 teaspoon (5 mL) sugar

Sea salt

Continued . . .

8. Heat ¼ cup (60 mL) olive oil in a large frying pan on medium heat and cook the polenta fries in two batches, being careful not to crowd the pan. Turn the fries when they are crispy and golden brown on each side (3 to 5 minutes per side), adding half of the chopped rosemary halfway through cooking each batch (if you add it too early, it will burn). Transfer the fries to a plate lined with paper towel to drain. Add more olive oil to the pan if needed, and repeat with the remaining fries.

9. Transfer the Rosemary Polenta Fries to a platter, sprinkle with salt to taste, and garnish with the rosemary sprigs. Serve immediately with the warm Smoky Tomato Dip on the side.

VEGAN: Use vegan butter and Vegan Parm (page 314).

GLUTEN-FREE: Use gluten-free vegetable stock.

COCONUT CAULIFLOWER TACOS
WITH PINEAPPLE SALSA

Makes 12 small tacos

This dish has to be one of our absolute favourites in this book. Coconut prawns take us right back to the shores of Maui on our family vacations, but this cauliflower version is without a doubt just as good! In fact, it was preferred over the prawns when tested by our meat-eating family. These tacos hit it out of the park in the flavour department with layers of crisp coconut-coated cauliflower, an addictive pineapple salsa, and a drizzle of spicy lime garlic aioli to round it all out. It's like sending your taste buds on a trip to Hawaii with every bite! This is a perfect meal to prepare for people with doubts about eating more plant-based foods. We promise it will not disappoint. This makes a lot of salsa: we love drowning our tacos in it (you'll understand as soon as you try it). Store any extra salsa in a covered container in the fridge for a couple of days.

1. MAKE THE PINEAPPLE SALSA In a large bowl, combine the pineapple, cilantro, red pepper, red onion, jalapeño, garlic, olive oil, lime juice, and salt. Stir well and set aside.

2. MAKE THE SPICY LIME GARLIC AIOLI In a small bowl, stir together the vegan mayonnaise, lime juice, Sriracha, and garlic. Set aside.

3. MAKE THE COCONUT CAULIFLOWER Rinse the cauliflower (if not previously washed) and lay it out on paper towels, blotting to remove extra moisture.

4. Place the coconut milk in one shallow bowl and the cornstarch in another shallow bowl. In a third shallow bowl, stir together the coconut, panko crumbs, and salt.

5. Working with one cauliflower floret at a time, coat the florets in the cornstarch (shaking off the excess), then dip in the coconut milk, followed by coating in the coconut and panko mixture. As they're coated, transfer to a baking sheet. Repeat until all the cauliflower florets are coated.

Pineapple Salsa

2 cups (500 mL) finely diced fresh pineapple

1 cup (250 mL) chopped fresh cilantro

1 cup (250 mL) finely diced sweet red pepper

¼ cup (60 mL) finely chopped red onion

½ jalapeño pepper, seeded and minced

2 cloves garlic, crushed

3 tablespoons (45 mL) extra-virgin olive oil

2 tablespoons (30 mL) fresh lime juice

½ teaspoon (2 mL) salt

Spicy Lime Garlic Aioli

¾ cup (175 mL) vegan mayonnaise

2 tablespoons (30 mL) fresh lime juice

1 tablespoon (15 mL) Sriracha

1 clove garlic, crushed

Continued...

6. Heat about 2 inches (5 cm) of avocado oil in a large, deep frying pan or shallow pot over medium-high heat. You can also use a deep-fryer. Either way, the oil should be about 350°F (180°C). Line a plate with paper towel or parchment paper.

7. Fry the cauliflower florets in small batches (being careful not to over-crowd the pan) until golden brown on all sides. Using a slotted spoon, transfer them to the paper towel–lined plate. Repeat until all the florets are cooked. You may need to scoop out any coconut that sinks to the bottom so it does not burn.

8. ASSEMBLE THE COCONUT CAULIFLOWER TACOS Heat the corn tortillas, one by one, in a hot dry cast-iron pan, 20 to 30 seconds per side, until soft and warm. (Or, using long metal tongs hold the tortillas, one by one, over an open flame of a gas range until the edges are slightly charred, 10 to 15 seconds per side.)

9. Place a couple of cauliflower florets in the centre of each tortilla. Top with Pineapple Salsa, Spicy Lime Garlic Aioli, avocado, cilantro, and jalapeños (if using). Serve with lime wedges.

GLUTEN-FREE: Use certified gluten-free coconut.

Coconut Cauliflower

1 large head cauliflower, cut into small florets

½ cup (125 mL) canned full-fat coconut milk

1 cup (250 mL) cornstarch

1 cup (250 mL) unsweetened shredded coconut

1 cup (250 mL) panko crumbs

1 teaspoon (5 mL) salt

Avocado oil (or other oil with a high smoke point), for frying

Tacos

12 small soft corn tortillas

2 avocados, pitted, peeled, and diced

1 bunch fresh cilantro, torn

Sliced jalapeño peppers (optional)

1 lime, cut into wedges

NACHO AVERAGE QUESO

Serves 10 to 12

Who doesn't love queso? Though it's typically loaded with cheese, this healthier plant-based version is every bit as delicious and perfect for game night or a Mexican-themed dinner. It's usually the first thing to disappear (even when served to non-vegans)! Nutritional yeast gives the dip its cheesy flavour; it's available at any health food store or in the natural foods section of the grocery store. You can buy chicken-flavoured vegetarian stock at many natural-health grocery stores, but you can use regular vegetable stock instead.

1. Soak the cashews in water for at least 4 hours or overnight (up to 12 hours) in the fridge. Drain and rinse before using (see Tip).

2. To roast the jalapeño pepper (or use pickled jalapeños and skip this step), preheat the oven to 425°F (220°C) and line a baking sheet with parchment paper. Cut off the jalapeño stem and roast the pepper on the baking sheet until the skin starts to blister, 15 to 20 minutes, turning partway through. Set aside to cool. Alternatively, roast your pepper on the open flame of a gas range, holding it with long tongs, until the skin is charred all over.

3. In a high-speed blender, combine the roasted or pickled jalapeño, cashews, nutritional yeast, beer, salsa, vegetarian stock, vegan butter, hot sauce, lime juice, cider vinegar, salt, chili powder, garlic powder, onion powder, cumin, and turmeric. Process on high until smooth and heated (if you have this option on your blender). The mixture should be thick but pourable; add more stock to thin if desired. If your blender does not have the heat option, simply warm the queso in the microwave or in a medium pot on the stove before serving.

4. Scrape the dip into a serving bowl, garnish with sliced jalapeños and fresh cilantro, and serve with tortilla chips.

TIP: The overnight soak works best, but if you don't have time to soak the cashews for several hours (or forgot), you can use the quick method: soak them in boiling water for 30 minutes, then drain and rinse.

GLUTEN-FREE: Use gluten-free beer, vegetable stock, spices, hot sauce, and tortilla chips.

1½ cups (375 mL) raw cashews

1 jalapeño pepper or 2 table-spoons (30 mL) pickled jalapeño peppers, more for garnish

⅔ cup (150 mL) nutritional yeast

½ cup (125 mL) lager or light beer

¼ cup (60 mL) your favourite salsa

¼ cup (60 mL) chicken-flavoured vegetarian stock, more to thin if needed

1 tablespoon (15 mL) vegan butter, melted

1 tablespoon (15 mL) hot sauce

Juice of 1 lime

1 teaspoon (5 mL) apple cider vinegar

1 teaspoon (5 mL) salt

½ teaspoon (2 mL) chili powder

½ teaspoon (2 mL) garlic powder

½ teaspoon (2 mL) onion powder

½ teaspoon (2 mL) ground cumin

¼ teaspoon (1 mL) turmeric

Fresh chopped cilantro, for garnish

Tortilla chips, for serving

FRESH SALSA AND GUACAMOLE

Serves 6 to 8

Our go-to summer appetizer is homemade salsa and guacamole served with a big bowl of the best tortilla chips you can get your hands on. This salsa is best made an hour or so before serving to allow the flavours to come together, but we recommend making the guacamole just before serving, as it will otherwise turn brown. You can add ingredients such as cilantro and diced tomato to the guacamole for extra flavour (we gave some options), but we love it plain and simple too without anything else added. We use the whole tomato in our salsa recipe (seeds and all, don't waste it!), but suggest draining the tomatoes to remove the extra liquid prior to making the salsa. This is a must-have for any taco or burrito night (try our Big Burritos on page 203); once you taste homemade salsa, you will never go back to the jarred version, we promise!

1. **MAKE THE FRESH SALSA** In a medium bowl, combine the tomatoes, cilantro, red onion, jalapeño, garlic, lime juice, olive oil, sugar, and salt to taste. Stir well. Refrigerate until ready to serve. The salsa is best served the same day, but can be made up to 1 day in advance.

2. **MAKE THE GUACAMOLE** Shortly before serving, mash the avocados with the lime juice and salt to taste in a medium bowl with a fork. Stir in the jalapeños, cilantro, and tomatoes (if using). Transfer to a small serving dish.

3. Serve with good-quality tortilla chips.

GLUTEN-FREE: Use gluten-free tortilla chips.

Fresh Salsa

2½ cups (575 mL) finely chopped tomatoes, drained in a sieve

1 cup (250 mL) chopped fresh cilantro

½ cup (125 mL) finely chopped red onion

½ to 1 jalapeño pepper (depending on how spicy you want it), seeds and membranes removed, finely chopped

2 cloves garlic, crushed

Juice of 2 limes

2 tablespoons (30 mL) extra-virgin olive oil

1 teaspoon (5 mL) sugar

Sea salt

Guacamole

2 large ripe avocados, pitted and peeled

Juice of 1 lime

Sea salt

1 teaspoon finely diced pickled jalapeños (optional)

2 tablespoons chopped fresh cilantro (optional)

¼ cup seeded diced tomatoes (optional)

Tortilla chips, for serving

SMOKED SALMON CAKES
WITH DILL TARTAR SAUCE

Serves 8 to 10

We created these salmon cakes for a recipe pairing for Sandhill wines, and they were a massive hit! Every time we make these, they are the first thing to be devoured, zero exceptions. You will want to make extra, trust us. The smoked salmon adds the most amazing flavour, and the dill tartar sauce is off-the-charts good. You can make smaller cakes using a smaller scoop and serve them as an appetizer, or make them as described and serve with a green salad (try our Great Green Salad on page 135) for a light lunch. Honestly, just try them and you'll see what we're talking about!

1. MAKE THE SALMON CAKES In a large bowl, combine both types of salmon, mayonnaise, mustard, red onion, dill, chives, capers, and 1 cup (250 mL) of the panko crumbs. Mix thoroughly. Season with salt and pepper, then mix in the eggs until combined.

2. Line a baking sheet with parchment paper. Place the remaining 2 cups (500 mL) panko crumbs on a large plate. Using a small ice cream scoop or your hands, form about 2 tablespoons (30 mL) of salmon mixture into a 3-inch (8 cm) round cake. Carefully place it on the pile of panko crumbs and gently press crumbs onto all sides of the cake. Using a metal spatula, carefully transfer the salmon cake to the prepared baking sheet. Repeat until all of the salmon mixture is used. Refrigerate the salmon cakes for 30 to 60 minutes so that they firm up (this will help them stay together when cooked).

3. MEANWHILE, MAKE THE DILL TARTAR SAUCE In a small bowl, combine the mayonnaise, dill pickle, red onion, dill, capers, and lemon juice. Stir until well mixed. Cover and refrigerate until ready to serve.

4. Line a large plate with paper towel. In a large frying pan, heat ½ inch (1 cm) avocado oil over medium-high heat. Working in batches, fry the salmon cakes, turning once, until golden brown on each side, 4 to 5 minutes per side. Using a metal spatula, transfer to the paper towel–lined plate. Repeat with the remaining salmon cakes. Serve hot with the Dill Tartar Sauce, garnished with fresh dill, if desired.

Salmon Cakes

1½ pounds (675 g) skinless wild salmon fillet cut into ¼-inch (5 mm) pieces (about 3 cups/750 mL)

7 ounces/200 g cold-smoked wild salmon cut into ¼-inch (5 mm) pieces (about 1 cup/250 mL)

¾ cup (175 mL) mayonnaise or vegan mayonnaise

1 teaspoon (5 mL) dry mustard

½ cup (125 mL) finely chopped red onion

½ cup (125 mL) finely chopped fresh dill, more for garnish

2 tablespoons (30 mL) thinly sliced fresh chives

3 tablespoons (45 mL) chopped drained capers

3 cups (750 mL) panko crumbs, divided

Salt and pepper

3 eggs, beaten

Avocado oil, for frying

Dill Tartar Sauce

¾ cup (175 mL) mayonnaise or vegan mayonnaise

¼ cup (60 mL) finely diced dill pickle

¼ cup (60 mL) finely chopped red onion

¼ cup (60 mL) chopped fresh dill, more for garnish

1 teaspoon (5 mL) drained capers, chopped

Juice of 1 lemon

TERRY'S BIG MUSSELS

Serves 4 to 6

When we were growing up, Tori's little brother Terry always wanted to be big and strong, and used to proclaim "I've got big muscles" while flexing his scrawny arms. Well, he got what he wished for: Terry outgrew us both (combined)! Turns out that our little brother is also a killer cook. Thanks for sharing your "big mussels" with us, Terry! These mussels are cooked in a perfectly balanced light cream sauce with a touch of heat from the curry paste and a briny zip thanks to the capers. They are a breeze to pull together. We love serving them for big casual get-togethers with plenty of bread to soak up all of the incredible sauce.

1. In a large frying pan or heavy-bottomed pot with a lid, heat the olive oil over medium heat. Add the shallots and cook until translucent and fragrant, about 2 minutes, stirring occasionally. Add the garlic and green onions and cook, stirring, for 1 minute.

2. Add the white wine and cook, stirring, until reduced by about one-third. Add the curry paste and cream and bring to a simmer while stirring to combine.

3. Add the mussels, tomatoes, and capers, cover with the lid, and cook until the mussels open up, 3 to 4 minutes. Remove from the heat and discard any mussels that haven't opened. Season with salt and pepper and serve immediately with sliced baguette.

DAIRY-FREE: Use canned full-fat coconut milk instead of cream.

- 2 tablespoons (30 mL) extra-virgin olive oil
- 2 medium shallots, finely chopped
- 3 cloves garlic, crushed
- 3 green onions (white and light green parts only), thinly sliced
- 1 cup (250 mL) white wine (we used pinot gris)
- 4 teaspoons (20 mL) green curry paste
- ¾ cup (175 mL) table (18%) cream or canned full-fat coconut milk
- 3 pounds (1.4 kg) fresh mussels, scrubbed and beards removed
- 2 medium tomatoes, seeded and diced
- 3 tablespoons (45 mL) capers (with the brine)
- Salt and pepper
- Sliced country loaf or baguette, for serving

SALADS & SOUPS

HEIRLOOM TOMATO FENNEL PANZANELLA

Serves 4 to 6

This tomato salad is our go-to in the later summer months when tomatoes are at their peak. Brimming with flavour, our favourite version of this classic Italian bread salad will have you coming back for more. The combo of the tomatoes, fennel, and bread is, well, perfection! We love using heirloom tomatoes from the market, but if all you can find is vine-ripened tomatoes, do not let that stop you from making this salad. Just choose the best-quality tomatoes you can get your hands on.

1. MAKE THE SALAD Preheat a grill to medium. Brush both sides of the baguette halves generously with olive oil and grill on both sides until lightly brown with grill marks. (Alternatively, toast under the broiler.) Transfer to a large platter, and once cool to the touch, roughly rub the cut side of the bread with the garlic halves and sprinkle lightly with sea salt. Tear the bread into large bite-size pieces.

2. In a large bowl, combine the tomatoes, chopped basil, fennel, and torn bread and toss to combine.

3. MAKE THE DRESSING In a small bowl, whisk together the olive oil, white wine vinegar, mustard, garlic, and salt to taste until emulsified. Pour the dressing over the salad and season with salt. Set aside at room temperature for 1 to 2 hours before serving, if possible, to allow the bread to absorb some of the dressing and the tomato juices. (But we have eaten it on the spot with no complaints!). Garnish with the licorice basil before serving.

Salad

1 baguette, halved lengthwise

Extra-virgin olive oil, for brushing the baguette

2 cloves garlic, halved

Sea salt

6 cups (1.5 L) roughly chopped heirloom tomatoes (about 1½-inch/4 cm pieces)

1 cup (250 mL) chopped fresh basil, for garnish

½ cup (125 mL) shaved fennel

Handful of fresh licorice basil (or regular basil), for garnish

Dressing

½ cup (125 mL) extra-virgin olive oil

2 tablespoons (30 mL) white wine vinegar

1 tablespoon (15 mL) Dijon mustard

2 cloves garlic, crushed

Salt

PICNIC PASTA SALAD

Serves 12 to 14

This recipe takes boring old-school macaroni salad (you know, the ones that give macaroni salad a bad name) and kicks it up a notch with a zippy dressing and extra veggies. Jillian made this for a family picnic and it was a favourite by a landslide—she always goes heavy on the pepper in this salad. The crunch of the veggies is a perfect contrast to the pasta and creamy dressing. This makes *a lot* of salad, so cut it in half if your crew is not as big (or as hungry!) as ours.

1. MAKE THE DRESSING In a small bowl, whisk together the vegan mayonnaise, white wine vinegar, sugar, lemon juice, Dijon mustard, dry mustard, onion powder, garlic powder, and salt and pepper to taste.

2. MAKE THE SALAD In a large pot of boiling salted water, cook the macaroni until just tender. Drain in a colander and rinse under cold water.

3. In a large serving bowl, combine the cooked pasta, red pepper, corn, cucumber, carrots, celery, parsley, and onion; toss to combine. Add the dressing, toss again to combine, and refrigerate until ready to serve. This salad can be made up to 1 day ahead and stored, covered, in the fridge.

GLUTEN-FREE: Use gluten-free pasta and mayonnaise.

Dressing

I cup (250 mL) vegan mayonnaise

3 tablespoons (45 mL) white wine vinegar

I tablespoon (15 mL) sugar

I tablespoon (15 mL) fresh lemon juice

I tablespoon (15 mL) Dijon mustard

I teaspoon (5 mL) dry mustard

½ teaspoon (2 mL) onion powder

½ teaspoon (2 mL) garlic powder

Salt and pepper

Salad

I pound (450 g) macaroni

I sweet red pepper, finely diced

I cup (250 mL) frozen corn, cooked and cooled

3 cups (750 mL) diced English cucumber (I medium cucumber)

I cup (250 mL) finely diced carrots

¾ cup (175 mL) diced celery

½ cup (125 mL) finely chopped fresh parsley

¼ cup (60 mL) finely chopped red onion

CAPTAIN'S KALE CAESAR SALAD

Serves 4

Justin, Jillian's fiancé, owns a boat-detailing company called Scrub Captain. When he first met Jillian, he made her this salad. We're pretty sure it's what sealed the deal—it was love at first bite! This salad is nothing short of amazing, there's something about the salty lemony dressing combined with the kale that blows any Caesar salad out of the water; we are all totally addicted to it and we're pretty sure you will be too. It is a hearty, zippy and healthier version of a Caesar salad with some easy tweaks if you want to make it vegan. If you want to take it the extra mile, serve it with Smoky Tofu Bacon (page 317).

1. MAKE THE DRESSING In a mason jar, combine the olive oil, Parmesan, mayonnaise, white wine vinegar, mustard, anchovy paste, Worcestershire sauce, garlic, lemon juice, and salt and pepper to taste. Seal the jar and shake vigorously until combined.

2. MAKE THE CROUTONS Heat the olive oil in a large frying pan over medium heat. Add as many baguette pieces as will fit in a single layer and sprinkle with salt to taste. Toast on each side, turning the bread with tongs or a spatula when each side is golden brown, 2 to 3 minutes per side. Transfer the croutons to a medium bowl and repeat with any remaining baguette pieces, adding more oil if needed.

3. ASSEMBLE THE SALAD Place the kale in a large salad bowl, add the dressing, croutons, and Parmesan, and toss well. Top with extra Parmesan and serve immediately.

VEGAN: Use vegan mayonnaise and Worcestershire sauce. Substitute 1 tablespoon (15 mL) minced capers for the anchovy paste and nutritional yeast or Vegan Parm (page 314) for the Parmesan cheese.

VEGETARIAN: Use 1 tablespoon (15 mL) minced capers instead of anchovy paste.

GLUTEN-FREE: Use gluten-free Worcestershire sauce and mayonnaise, and use gluten-free bread for the croutons.

Dressing

¼ cup (60 mL) extra-virgin olive oil

2 tablespoons (30 mL) grated Parmesan cheese or Vegan Parm (page 314)

2 tablespoons (30 mL) mayonnaise or vegan mayonnaise

1 tablespoon (15 mL) white wine vinegar

2 teaspoons (10 mL) Dijon mustard

2 teaspoons (10 mL) anchovy paste

½ teaspoon (2 mL) Worcestershire sauce

2 cloves garlic, crushed

Juice of 1 lemon

Salt and pepper

Croutons

3 tablespoons (45 mL) extra-virgin olive oil, more if needed

½ day-old baguette, torn into 1-inch (2.5 cm) pieces (about 3 cups/750 mL)

Sea salt

Salad

8 cups (2 L) lightly packed torn green curly kale with stems removed

¼ cup (60 mL) grated Parmesan cheese or Vegan Parm (page 314), more for serving

GRILLED VEGGIE ORZO SALAD

Serves 6

There is something so satisfying about a salad that is packed with colourful healthy vegetables and amazing Mediterranean flavours. This one is our summer staple. Whenever we make our Summer Herbed Grilled Vegetables (page 224) we double the recipe just so we can have this salad the next day. But this is an awesome way to use up any left-over grilled veggies (don't worry if you don't have the exact amount). We love that it can be made ahead of time for stress-free entertaining!

1. In a medium pot of boiling salted water, cook the orzo until just tender. Drain in a large sieve and rinse with cold water under the tap. Place it in a large serving bowl.

2. Add the grilled vegetables, basil, feta, olives, and red onion.

3. In a medium cup or jar with a tight fitting lid, whisk or shake together the olive oil, lemon juice, and red wine vinegar until emulsified. Season with salt and pepper. The dressing can be made 1 day ahead and stored in a resealable container in the fridge. Toss the salad with the dressing to combine and serve immediately.

VEGAN: Skip the feta cheese or use Vegan Feta (page 316 or store-bought).

GLUTEN-FREE: Substitute quinoa for the orzo.

2 cups (500 mL) orzo pasta

3 cups (750 mL) Summer Herbed Grilled Vegetables (page 224), diced

1 cup (250 mL) loosely packed fresh basil leaves, chopped

⅔ cup (150 mL) crumbled feta cheese

½ cup (125 mL) sliced green olives or chopped marinated artichoke hearts

¼ cup (60 mL) finely chopped red onion

2 tablespoons (30 mL) extra-virgin olive oil

2 tablespoons (30 mL) fresh lemon juice

1 tablespoon (15 mL) red wine vinegar

Salt and pepper

GREAT GREEN SALAD

Serves 4 to 6

There is nothing fancy about this salad but there is something magical about the dressing that gives life to any veggie you choose to throw at it. The dressing is a weekly staple at Tori's house and chances are, if you come for dinner, this dressing will be on the table. This salad is designed to let whatever seasonal vegetables you can get your hands on shine through. It's best in the summer, when gardens and farmers' markets are overflowing. Use your imagination when it comes to vegetables; the ones we list are merely suggestions. Tossing the salad in the dressing gives the best flavour and coverage, but you can serve it on the side to let your guests add as much or as little as they want. We often switch it up by topping the salad with toasted pumpkin seeds or sunflower seeds to add some extra crunch and protein. You will likely have some dressing left over, store it in the fridge in a reasealable container for 1 to 2 days.

1. MAKE THE DRESSING In a small, deep bowl or mason jar, combine the garlic, lemon juice, red wine vinegar, honey, and mustard. Whisk together or shake to combine. Slowly add the avocado oil while whisking until emulsified. If you are using a mason jar, add the oil with the other ingredients, seal the jar, and shake vigorously until emulsified. Season with salt and pepper.

2. ASSEMBLE THE SALAD Arrange the lettuce leaves on a platter and scatter the beet, cucumber, avocado, and onion on top. Serve the dressing on the side or toss it together with just enough dressing to coat the lettuce.

VEGAN: Use maple syrup instead of honey.

Dressing

2 cloves garlic, crushed

Juice of 1 lemon (about 2 tablespoons/30 mL)

3 tablespoons (45 mL) red wine vinegar

1 tablespoon (15 mL) pure liquid honey or maple syrup

2 teaspoons (10 mL) Dijon mustard

⅔ cup (150 mL) avocado oil or extra-virgin olive oil

Salt and pepper

Salad

1 head red or green lettuce, leaves separated (and torn into 1-inch/2.5 cm pieces, if desired)

1 small beet (any colour), peeled and thinly sliced

½ English cucumber, sliced

1 avocado, pitted, peeled, and sliced

¼ red onion, thinly sliced

HARVEST KALE SLAW WITH TAHINI DRESSING

Serves 4 to 6

After a fun-filled three-day girls' trip to Hawaii with a red-eye flight back home, we ended up at Heirloom, a Vancouver eatery known for their unbelievable vegetarian food. We ordered their kale salad to share, and we all fought for the last bite. Back in Kelowna, our team member and friend Mackenzie whipped up this version for us, and she nailed it! This one is so unique, delicious, and healthy! You will not use all the dressing, so store the extra in a resealable container in the fridge for up to 1 week.

1. MAKE THE TAHINI DRESSING In a blender (or deep, narrow container if using an immersion blender), combine the garlic, nutritional yeast, tahini, tamari, cider vinegar, lemon juice, maple syrup, water, and avocado oil. Blend for 2 minutes, or until smooth.

2. MAKE THE HARVEST KALE SLAW In a large bowl, combine the kale, cabbage, carrots, red onion, sunflower seeds, pumpkin seeds, and cranberries. Toss to combine and set aside.

3. Press the tofu cubes between 2 sheets of paper towel or a kitchen towel to remove any extra moisture.

4. In a small bowl, sprinkle the tofu cubes with the cornstarch and toss to coat. Shake off any excess.

5. In a small frying pan, heat the olive oil over medium heat. Lightly fry the tofu cubes until they are light golden on all sides, about 2 minutes in total. Remove from the heat and transfer the tofu to a plate to cool.

6. Slowly pour the Tahini Dressing over the Harvest Kale Slaw, adding just enough to coat the salad or to taste (you will not use all the dressing). Add the tofu, toss again, and serve immediately.

Tahini Dressing

2 cloves garlic, crushed

⅓ cup (75 mL) nutritional yeast

¼ cup (60 mL) tahini

3 tablespoons + 1½ teaspoons (52 mL) tamari

2 tablespoons (30 mL) apple cider vinegar

1 tablespoon (15 mL) fresh lemon juice

½ teaspoon (2 mL) pure maple syrup

½ cup (125 mL) water

¼ cup (60 mL) avocado, grapeseed oil or other neutral-tasting oil

Harvest Kale Slaw

4 cups (1 L) lightly packed finely chopped green curly kale with stems removed

3 cups (750 mL) shredded red cabbage

1½ cups (375 mL) grated carrots (2 to 3 large carrots)

⅓ cup (75 mL) finely chopped red onion

½ cup (125 mL) sunflower seeds

½ cup (125 mL) pumpkin seeds

½ cup (125 mL) dried cranberries

1 package (7½ ounces/210 g) smoked extra-firm tofu, cut into ½-inch (1 cm) cubes

1 tablespoon (15 mL) cornstarch

2 tablespoons (30 mL) extra-virgin olive oil

MEXICAN KALE SALAD
WITH AVOCADO LIME DRESSING

Serves 6 to 8

This salad is on constant rotation at Tori's house: we are all a bit obsessed! It is super hearty with all of the Mexican flavours we love, and it keeps well to pack as lunch the following day if you have any leftovers. We like serving it with crushed tortilla chips to add some crunch. Use as much or as little jalapeño pepper as you like or can handle.

1. MAKE THE AVOCADO LIME DRESSING In a small blender (or medium bowl if using an immersion blender), combine the avocado, garlic, jalapeño, cilantro, olive oil, lime juice, honey, white wine vinegar, mustard, and salt to taste. Blend on medium speed until smooth.

2. MAKE THE MEXICAN KALE SALAD In a large bowl, combine the kale, sweet peppers, tomatoes, cilantro, cucumber, feta, green onion, jalapeño (if using), black beans, corn, and Avocado Lime Dressing. Toss well. Serve with a handful of the tortilla chips on top (if using) for extra crunch!

Avocado Lime Dressing

1 large avocado, pitted and peeled

1 clove garlic, crushed

½ jalapeño pepper, seeds and membranes removed

1 cup (250 mL) loosely packed fresh cilantro

⅔ cup (150 mL) extra-virgin olive oil

3 tablespoons (45 mL) fresh lime juice

2 tablespoons (30 mL) pure liquid honey or maple syrup

1 tablespoon (15 mL) white wine vinegar

2 teaspoons (10 mL) Dijon mustard

Salt

Mexican Kale Salad

6 cups (1.5 L) lightly packed torn green curly kale leaves with stems removed

2 cups (500 mL) diced sweet yellow, orange, and/or red peppers

2 cups (500 mL) diced tomatoes

2 cups (500 mL) lightly packed chopped fresh cilantro (about 2 bunches)

2 cups (500 mL) diced English cucumber

1 cup (250 mL) crumbled feta cheese or Vegan Feta (page 316)

½ cup (125 mL) sliced green onion

1 to 2 tablespoons (15 to 30 mL) finely diced seeded jalapeño pepper (optional)

1 can (19 ounces/540 mL) black beans, drained and rinsed

1 cup (250 mL) canned or frozen corn kernels, cooked and cooled

Crushed tortilla chips, for serving (optional)

VEGAN: Use Vegan Feta (page 316 or store-bought) instead of feta cheese or skip it. Use maple syrup or organic cane sugar instead of honey in the dressing.

GLUTEN-FREE: Use gluten-free tortilla chips.

GRANNY'S BORSCHT

Serves 8 to 10

Our granny has always been ahead of the curve. Chickpea brownies? She was all over it years ago, long before it was hip. Vegan borscht? Yeah, she had that covered too. Her borscht is so simple and it's *the best!* When Granny makes a big pot we all go scurrying over for a bowl—it is not to be missed.

Do not wear clothes you really care about when making this soup—it's messy and the beets stain. Granny uses a mandoline to julienne the beets, which saves loads of time, but you can dice them by hand if you like. Be sure to season well with salt before serving or it will taste bland. Granny always served it with a splash of whipping cream, for the record.

1. Place the beets, carrots, and onion in a large pot. Cover with the water, bring to a boil, then reduce the heat and simmer until the vegetables are fork-tender, about 35 minutes.

2. Remove from the heat and stir in the peas, dill, and salt to taste. Divide the soup among bowls and serve. Store, covered, in the fridge for up to 5 days or in the freezer for up to 1 month.

4 cups (1 L) peeled red beets julienned on a mandoline or cut into ½-inch (1 cm) cubes

2 cups (500 mL) peeled carrots cut into ½-inch (1 cm) cubes

1 small yellow onion, finely chopped

12 cups (3 L) water

2 cups (500 mL) frozen peas

¾ cup (175 mL) chopped fresh dill

Salt

ROASTED ROOT VEGGIE SOUP

Serves 8

We always keep this soup on standby for a post-Thanksgiving dinner; it is such a creative way to use up leftover roasted veggies. It is smooth, creamy, packed with autumn flavours, *and* vegan and gluten-free! You can serve it with a drizzle of Cashew Cream (page 313), but it is awesome just on its own. Tori used to make this almost weekly for Jillian when we lived across the street from each other, to help recover from weekends packed with just a *bit* too much fun. The nutritional yeast is optional, but gives the soup a slightly cheesy flavour. Jillian claims this soup cannot be served without our biscuits (page 235), so get crackin', you have two recipes to make!

1. In a large, heavy-bottomed pot, heat the olive oil over medium heat. Add the onion and celery and cook until the onions are soft and translucent, about 5 minutes, stirring occasionally. Add the garlic and cook for 2 minutes, stirring.

2. Add the Roasted Root Veggies and vegetable stock. Bring to a simmer, then reduce the heat to medium-low and cook, stirring occasionally, until the vegetables are soft, 30 to 45 minutes.

3. Using an immersion blender, purée the soup until smooth and creamy. Thin with additional stock, if needed. Stir in the nutritional yeast (if using), and season with salt and pepper.

4. Divide soup among bowls. Garnish with a swirl of Cashew Cream (if using) and a sprig of fresh thyme, and serve.

2 tablespoons (30 mL) extra-virgin olive oil

2 cups (500 mL) roughly chopped yellow onion

2 cups (500 mL) roughly chopped celery

4 cloves garlic, crushed

1 batch Roasted Root Veggies (page 222)

8 cups (2 L) vegetable stock, more if needed

⅓ cup (75 mL) nutritional yeast (optional)

Salt and pepper

Cashew Cream (page 313), for serving (optional)

8 sprigs fresh thyme, for garnish

GLUTEN-FREE: Use gluten-free vegetable stock.

FRENCH ONION SOUP WITH THYME CROUTONS

Serves 6

French onion soup is pure wizardry if you ask us. There's really no better dish to serve on a cozy fall day. You can leave the cheese out completely. It will be a different experience altogether, but still delicious. Just skip the broiling step!

1. START THE FRENCH ONION SOUP In a large, heavy-bottomed pot, heat the olive oil and butter over medium-low heat. Add the onions and garlic and cook until the onions are soft and translucent, 5 to 8 minutes, stirring occasionally.

2. Stir in the chopped thyme. Reduce the heat to low and continue to cook, stirring occasionally, until the onions are light golden brown, about 30 minutes.

3. MEANWHILE, MAKE THE THYME CROUTONS Preheat the oven to 350°F (180°C). Line a baking sheet with parchment paper.

4. Place the bread cubes in a large bowl. In a small bowl, stir together the olive oil, thyme, rosemary, salt, and garlic. Pour over the baguette cubes and toss to coat.

5. Spread the baguette cubes evenly on the prepared baking sheet. Sprinkle the Parmesan over the bread and toss with your hands to coat. Spread evenly again. Bake, tossing occasionally with a wooden spoon, until golden brown, 20 to 30 minutes. Let cool.

6. FINISH THE SOUP To the onions, add the red wine and cook over medium heat for 3 to 5 minutes, stirring occasionally. Add the vegetable stock and season with salt and pepper.

7. Meanwhile, preheat the broiler to medium-high.

8. Place 6 heatproof onion soup bowls on a baking sheet and ladle in the soup. Place a handful of Thyme Croutons on top of each bowl and immediately top with a handful of the Gruyère and a sprig of thyme. Broil until the cheese starts to bubble and turn brown. Serve immediately.

VEGAN: Use vegan butter. Leave out the cheese and skip the broiling step. Serve the soup with a handful of croutons.

GLUTEN-FREE: Use gluten-free vegetable stock and bread to make the croutons.

French Onion Soup

- 2 tablespoons (30 mL) extra-virgin olive oil
- 1 tablespoon (15 mL) butter or vegan butter
- 6 large yellow onions, thinly sliced
- 2 cloves garlic, crushed
- ½ cup (125 mL) roughly chopped fresh thyme
- ¾ cup (175 mL) good-quality dry red wine (we use merlot)
- 8 cups (2 L) vegetable stock
- Salt and pepper
- 1½ cups (375 mL) grated Gruyère cheese
- 6 sprigs fresh thyme, for garnish

Thyme Croutons

- 1 day-old baguette, cut into ½-inch (1 cm) cubes
- ¼ cup (60 mL) extra-virgin olive oil
- 2 teaspoons (10 mL) chopped fresh thyme
- 2 teaspoons (10 mL) chopped fresh rosemary
- ½ teaspoon (2 mL) salt
- 1 clove garlic, crushed
- 3 tablespoons (45 mL) grated Parmesan cheese

CREAM OF MUSHROOM SOUP

Serves 6

Mushroom soup has long been one of Jillian's favourite soups, and she is still a huge mushroom fan. (Thank you, Granny, for handing down your love of mushrooms to us!) We tested this recipe with a variety of mushrooms—brown, white, chanterelles, and morels—and all worked well. When Jillian first started making mushroom soup, it was a big hit. It wasn't vegan, but since then she has replaced the cream and butter with plant-based ingredients. Today, it is still a huge hit in Jillian's house, and she's proud to bring it to the table knowing it's completely plant-based. This creamy soup is delicious served with sliced baguette brushed with olive oil and toasted. See the Tip below if you like smaller bits of mushrooms in your soup.

1. In a medium, heavy-bottomed pot, heat the olive oil and vegan butter over medium-low heat. Once the butter has melted, add the onion and cook until soft and translucent, 5 to 8 minutes, stirring occasionally. Add the garlic and cook, stirring, for 30 seconds.

2. Stir in the white wine, thyme, nutmeg, and mushrooms. Cook, stirring occasionally, until the mushrooms soften, 7 to 9 minutes. Stir in the parsley and cook for 1 minute. Stir in the vegetable stock and Cashew Cream and simmer until it is hot. Thin with extra stock as needed. Season with salt and pepper.

3. Divide soup among bowls and serve.

- 1 tablespoon (15 mL) extra-virgin olive oil
- 1 tablespoon (15 mL) vegan butter
- ½ cup (125 mL) finely chopped yellow onion (1 small onion)
- 1 large clove garlic, crushed
- ½ cup (125 mL) white wine (we use pinot gris)
- 1 teaspoon (5 mL) fresh thyme leaves
- Pinch of nutmeg
- 10 ounces (285 g) chopped mushrooms (4 cups/1 L)
- ¼ cup (60 mL) finely chopped fresh flat-leaf parsley
- 3 cups (750 mL) vegetable stock, more to thin if needed
- 1½ cups (375 mL) Cashew Cream (page 313)
- Salt and pepper

GLUTEN-FREE: Use gluten-free vegetable stock and skip the baguette or serve with gluten-free bread.

TIP: If you prefer smaller mushroom pieces in your soup, after step 2 transfer half of the soup into a tall medium-sized bowl and purée with an immersion blender to reach the desired consistency. Return the puréed soup to the pot. Stir and serve.

CREAMY ROASTED TOMATO BASIL SOUP
WITH GARLIC CROUTONS

Serves 8

Tomato soup is the food equivalent of a warm hug, and this one ticks all the boxes and then some. It is easy, can be made at any time of year (though the end of summer is best, when tomatoes are falling off the vines), and is vegan and gluten-free (if you skip the croutons). Oh yes, and it tastes *amazing*! Roasting the tomatoes with the onions brings out the best in these vegetables—there is some serious flavour hiding in there! Puréeing the soup gives it a creamy texture and taste without a single drop of cream.

1. Preheat the oven to 325°F (160°C). Line a baking sheet with parchment paper.

2. MAKE THE GARLIC CROUTONS Spread the baguette pieces on the baking sheet. Drizzle the olive oil over the bread, sprinkle it with the salt, and add the crushed garlic. Gently massage it all together with your hands. Bake until the croutons are golden brown, tossing halfway through baking, 13 to 18 minutes. Set aside.

3. MAKE THE CREAMY ROASTED TOMATO BASIL SOUP Increase the oven temperature to 400°F (200°C). Line a separate baking sheet with parchment paper.

4. Cut the tomatoes in half lengthwise and place them cut side up on the prepared baking sheet. Cut one onion into wedges and add to the tomatoes. Drizzle everything with ¼ cup (60 mL) of the olive oil. Sprinkle with the salt, then gently massage the oil and salt into the tomatoes and onions. Evenly space them out on the baking sheet, making sure the tomatoes are cut side up. Roast for 1 hour.

5. When the tomatoes and onions are done, roughly chop the remaining onion. Heat the remaining 2 tablespoons (30 mL) olive oil in a medium, heavy-bottomed pot over medium heat. Add the chopped onion and cook until soft and translucent, 3 to 5 minutes, stirring occasionally. Add the garlic and cook, stirring, until the garlic is fragrant, about 1 minute. Add the white wine and cook, stirring occasionally, until reduced by half, about 5 minutes. Add the roasted tomatoes and onions (along with any juices from the baking sheet), the tomato paste, and vegetable stock. Bring to a simmer and cook for 30 minutes, stirring occasionally.

Garlic Croutons

5 cups (1.25 L) cubed or roughly torn bite-size pieces of day-old baguette

¼ cup (60 mL) extra-virgin olive oil

½ teaspoon (2 mL) sea salt

2 cloves garlic, crushed

Creamy Roasted Tomato Basil Soup

2 pounds (900 g) Roma tomatoes (about 10 tomatoes)

2 large sweet yellow onions, divided

¼ cup (60 mL) + 2 tablespoons (30 mL) extra-virgin olive oil, divided

½ teaspoon (2 mL) sea salt

4 cloves garlic, crushed

½ cup (125 mL) dry white wine (we use pinot gris)

2 tablespoons (30 mL) tomato paste

4 cups (1 L) vegetable stock

½ cup (125 mL) finely chopped fresh basil, more for garnish

6. Stir in the basil and cook for 5 minutes. Remove from the heat and purée with an immersion blender until smooth and creamy. (Or cool the soup slightly and blend in a high-speed blender.) Reheat if needed.

7. Divide soup among bowls, top with a handful of Garlic Croutons and a sprinkle of chopped basil, and serve.

GLUTEN-FREE: Use gluten-free stock and bread to make the croutons or leave them out.

MAIN DISHES

BUTTERNUT SQUASH CARBONARA

Serves 4 to 6

Carbonara—so yummy, you're thinking, but *so* sinful. Not so fast! We kicked out the bacon and cream to make this classic dish much healthier, yet it's still incredibly smooth and velvety thanks to the butternut squash and the pasta water. Butternut squash is so flavourful (and healthy!). The natural sweetness and flavour are really brought out when cooked with the garlic and onion, and it purées into the silkiest sauce that will throw your taste buds for a loop! Never throw out your pasta water before serving your pasta: it is the best way to loosen up the pasta and add a velvety texture without adding more fat.

¼ cup (60 mL) extra-virgin olive oil

12 fresh sage leaves

1½ cups (375 mL) finely chopped yellow onion (about 1 medium onion)

3 cloves garlic, crushed

3½ cups (875 mL) peeled and diced butternut squash

1½ cups (375 mL) vegetable stock

¼ cup (60 mL) nutritional yeast

⅔ cup (150 mL) grated Parmesan cheese or Vegan Parm (page 314), more for serving

Salt and pepper

12 ounces (340 g) linguine

1. Heat the olive oil in a medium, heavy-bottomed frying pan over medium heat. Add the sage leaves and cook until crispy, about 2 minutes. Use a slotted spoon or tongs to transfer the sage leaves to a small plate and set aside.

2. Add the onions to the pan and cook over medium heat until soft and translucent, 3 to 5 minutes, stirring occasionally. Add the garlic and cook for 30 seconds, stirring occasionally. Add the butternut squash and the vegetable stock, stir, cover, and simmer until the squash is very soft, 20 to 25 minutes.

3. Meanwhile, bring a large pot of salted water to a boil for the pasta.

4. Transfer the butternut squash mixture to a medium, deep bowl and, using an immersion blender, blend until smooth (be careful not to burn yourself). Return the squash mixture to the pan and add 6 fried sage leaves, nutritional yeast, Parmesan, and salt and pepper to taste.

5. Add the pasta to the boiling water and cook until just tender.

6. Using tongs, add the cooked pasta to the butternut squash mixture along with ½ cup (125 mL) of the pasta water. Stir together with the tongs, adding more pasta water if needed to make a smooth, velvety sauce. Season with additional salt and pepper, if needed.

7. Divide the pasta among pasta dishes and garnish with extra Parmesan and the remaining 6 fried sage leaves. Serve immediately.

VEGAN: Use Vegan Parm (page 314).

GLUTEN-FREE: Use gluten-free vegetable stock and pasta.

SPRING ORECCHIETTE

Serves 4

Nothing says spring like asparagus! This pasta is a breeze to throw together for last-minute company or a weeknight meal. It is so gorgeous and fresh tasting with a hint of lemon; it's all kinds of gourmet without any of the fuss. You can use any medium-sized pasta, like rotini or penne, if you cannot find orecchiette. We prefer thinner asparagus for this dish if you can find it. Save some of the pasta water to add at the end if your pasta dries out. It's the best trick in the book and will give you an incredibly velvety pasta every time.

1. Bring a large pot of well-salted water to a boil. Add the pasta and cook until just tender, 10 to 12 minutes. Drain in a colander and set aside.

2. Meanwhile, in a large frying pan heat the olive oil over medium heat. Add the shallot and cook, stirring occasionally, until translucent and just starting to turn golden, 3 to 4 minutes. Add the white wine and cook until reduced by half, stirring occasionally.

3. Add the asparagus and cook for 2 minutes. Stir in the peas, parsley, vegetable stock, and lemon zest and cook until the peas are bright green and tender, about 4 minutes. Add the cooked pasta, arugula, and Parmesan, and toss together until the arugula is just wilted. Season with salt and pepper, and add the goat cheese in small pieces.

4. Divide the pasta among pasta dishes and top with extra Parmesan, if desired. Serve immediately.

VEGAN: Use Vegan Parm (page 314) and substitute cashew cheese (an herb flavour will work as well) for goat cheese.

GLUTEN-FREE: Use gluten-free pasta and vegetable stock.

⅔ pound (300 g) orecchiette

3 tablespoons (45 mL) extra-virgin olive oil

½ cup (125 mL) finely chopped shallot (1 large shallot)

½ cup (125 mL) white wine (we use pinot gris)

2 cups (500 mL) trimmed asparagus cut into 2-inch (5 cm) lengths (1 bunch of asparagus)

1 cup (250 mL) frozen peas

¼ cup (60 mL) finely chopped fresh flat-leaf parsley

½ cup (125 mL) vegetable stock or chicken-flavoured vegetarian stock

1 teaspoon (5 mL) packed grated fresh lemon zest

3 cups (750 mL) lightly packed baby arugula

¼ cup (60 mL) grated Parmesan cheese or Vegan Parm (page 314), more for serving

Salt and pepper

⅓ cup (75 mL) plain goat cheese or spreadable cashew cheese

PINK PASTA

Serves 4

Team Jilly created this pasta for Valentine's Day one year, and it was a huge hit! The roasted beets give this showy pasta such a gorgeous pink colour and a rich flavour. The blended cashews add a creamy texture to the dish while the lemon juice brightens the dish to balance it out. You can use whatever pasta shape you wish. This recipe is a good one to pull out when you are looking for something different to serve your guests. Serve it with a glass of rosé . . . of course!

1. Soak the cashews in water for at least 4 hours or overnight (up to 12 hours) in the fridge. Drain and rinse before using (see Tip).

2. Preheat the oven to 425°F (220°C).

3. Place the beet cubes on a small piece of foil, drizzle with olive oil, and sprinkle with salt. Close up the foil and roast for 50 to 60 minutes, until fork-tender.

4. In a high-speed blender, combine the cashews, garlic, water, lemon juice, and salt to taste. Add one piece of beet and blend on high speed. Add more beet pieces, one at a time, to reach the level of pink colour or beet flavour you desire (we only added 1 or 2 pieces), blending on high speed until smooth, about 2 minutes.

5. Bring a large pot of well-salted water to a boil. Add the pasta and cook until just tender, 9 to 13 minutes. Reserve ⅔ cup (150 mL) or more of the pasta water and drain the pasta.

6. Meanwhile, heat a large frying pan over medium heat. Add the cashew beet sauce and bring to a simmer. Reduce the heat to low, stir in the white wine, ⅓ cup (75 mL) of the reserved pasta water, and vegetable stock, and simmer until warmed through. Taste and adjust seasoning.

7. Add the pasta to the cashew beet sauce and toss with tongs until fully coated. Add a bit more of the reserved pasta water if the sauce is too thick.

8. Divide the pasta among pasta dishes, top with Vegan Parm, and serve immediately.

GLUTEN-FREE: Use gluten-free pasta and vegetable stock.

¾ cup (175 mL) raw cashews (see Tip)

1 small red beet, peeled and cut into 1-inch (2.5 cm) cubes

1 tablespoon (15 mL) extra-virgin olive oil

¼ teaspoon (1 mL) salt

2 cloves garlic

¾ cup (175 mL) water

2 tablespoons (30 mL) fresh lemon juice

⅓ cup (75 mL) dry white wine or rosé wine (we use rosé)

¼ cup (60 mL) vegetable stock

9 ounces (250 g) fettuccine

Vegan Parm (page 314), for serving

TIP: The overnight soak works best, but if you don't have time to soak the cashews for several hours (or forgot), you can use the quick method: soak them in boiling water for 30 minutes, then drain and rinse.

GARDEN BOLOGNESE

Serves 4 to 6

This dish is a family favourite, and even our meat-loving dads go crazy over it. The sauce is rich, hearty and so satisfying and basically everything one could hope for in a pasta sauce. We chop the veggies very fine so that they almost disappear into the sauce. You can skip chopping by hand, and like us, use a food processor instead (see Tip). This works really well! Simply fire them in the food processor whole! It not only makes for a better texture, but unsuspecting kids will have zero clue how healthy it is—mom win! The sauce freezes nicely. We always kick ourselves for not making a double batch.

1. Heat 2 tablespoons (30 mL) of the olive oil in a large frying pan over medium heat. Add the onions, carrots, and celery. Cook until the onions are soft and translucent, 4 to 5 minutes, stirring occasionally.

2. In another large frying pan over medium heat, melt the vegan butter in the remaining 2 tablespoons (30 mL) olive oil. Add the mushrooms and cook until they are soft and begin to brown, 5 to 10 minutes, stirring occasionally.

3. Add the garlic and cook, stirring, for 1 minute. Add the red wine and continue to cook until the wine is reduced by half, stirring with a wooden spatula, scraping the bottom of the pan. Add the tomato paste, stock concentrate, and water and stir.

4. Add the cooked onion mixture, tomatoes with their juice, nutritional yeast, oregano, basil, and fennel. Reduce the heat to medium-low heat and cook, stirring occasionally, until reduced and thick, 20 to 30 minutes. If it is too thick, add more stock and water; if it is too thin, continue to reduce.

5. Add the red wine vinegar and season with salt and pepper. Simmer for another 5 minutes. Stir in the Cashew Cream.

6. Meanwhile, bring a large pot of well-salted water to a boil. Add the pasta and cook until just tender, 8 to 12 minutes. Drain.

7. Divide the pasta among pasta dishes. Pour the sauce over the pasta and serve immediately with Vegan Parm on the side.

GLUTEN-FREE: Use gluten-free pasta and stock concentrate.

NUT-FREE: Use soy creamer instead of Cashew Cream.

4 tablespoons (60 mL) extra-virgin olive oil, divided

2 cups (500 mL) finely chopped yellow onion (1 large onion)

1 cup (250 mL) very finely chopped peeled carrots

1 cup (250 mL) very finely chopped celery (3 stalks)

2 tablespoons (30 mL) vegan butter

1¼ pounds (565 g) brown and/or portobello mushrooms, very finely chopped (6 cups/1.5 L; see Tip)

3 cloves garlic, crushed

½ cup (125 mL) red wine (we use cabernet merlot)

1 can (5½ ounces/156 mL) tomato paste

4 teaspoons (20 mL) beef-flavoured vegetarian stock concentrate

2 cups (500 mL) water

1 can (28 ounces/796 mL) diced tomatoes

½ cup (125 mL) nutritional yeast

1 tablespoon (15 mL) dried oregano

1 tablespoon (15 mL) dried basil

1 tablespoon + 1 teaspoon (20 mL) fennel seeds, finely ground

1½ teaspoons (7 mL) red wine vinegar

Salt and pepper

¼ cup (60 mL) Cashew Cream (page 313) or soy creamer

18 ounces (500 g) bucatini or spaghetti

Vegan Parm (page 314), for serving

TIP: 1. Instead of chopping the vegetables, you can process them separately in a food processor in batches. This will give the sauce a very meaty texture. 2. Use regular vegetable stock if you cannot find beef-flavoured vegetarian stock.

LIME CAPELLINI

Serves 4

Our friend Charles (not to be confused with Tori's husband) made this pasta for Tori at his house in Brazil. There were many amazing things Tori came home with from that trip—including a killer tan and a number of way-too-skimpy bikinis—but this pasta tops them all! It is bright, zingy, and perfect just as is. This pasta comes together quickly, so have all your ingredients ready and your pot of water boiling before starting the sauce.

1. Bring a large pot of well-salted water to a boil.

2. In a large, deep, heavy-bottomed frying pan, heat the olive oil over medium heat. Add the shallots and cook until soft and translucent, 2 to 3 minutes, stirring occasionally. Add the garlic and cook, stirring, until translucent and fragrant, about 1 minute, being careful not to brown the garlic.

3. Add the white wine, increase the heat to medium-high, and cook until the wine is reduced by half, 3 to 5 minutes. Remove from the heat.

4. Meanwhile, add the pasta to the boiling water and cook until just tender, 3 to 5 minutes. Reserve 1 cup (250 mL) of the pasta water.

5. Using tongs, transfer the pasta to the frying pan. Add the lime zest, lime juice, parsley, Parmesan, and salt, to taste. Toss gently with the tongs to combine. Add the reserved pasta water ¼ cup (60 mL) at a time, tossing until the pasta is loose and velvety.

6. Divide the pasta among pasta dishes and top with extra Parmesan and parsley. Serve immediately.

3 tablespoons (45 mL) extra-virgin olive oil

¼ cup (60 mL) finely chopped shallot (1 medium shallot)

2 large cloves garlic, minced

1 cup (250 mL) dry white wine (we use sauvignon blanc)

14 ounces (400 g) capellini

4 teaspoons (20 mL) grated fresh lime zest (from 2 limes)

2 tablespoons (30 mL) fresh lime juice (from 2 limes)

1 cup (250 mL) loosely packed chopped fresh flat-leaf parsley, more for serving

⅔ cup (150 mL) grated Parmesan cheese or Vegan Parm (page 314), more for serving

Salt

VEGAN: Use Vegan Parm (page 314).

GLUTEN-FREE: Use gluten-free pasta.

EAT-YOUR-VEGGIES PASTA

Serves 6 to 8

You *can* have your cake and eat it too. Or at least your pasta, when it's piled with veggies! We're all for pasta that doesn't leave you feeling heavy and reaching for a pillow, like this light, veggie-infused one. A simple white wine sauce gives this colourful pasta tons of flavour, and the feta (should you choose to add it) really rounds out the dish. Use your imagination with the vegetables—so long as the ratios are the same, you can experiment with whatever you have on hand. This pasta is inspired by a local restaurant called Ricardo's Mediterranean Kitchen, in Lake Country, B.C., that is a stone's throw from where we all used to camp on Kalamalka Lake when we were kids. Our summers were filled with cliff-jumping into crystal-clear blue-green water, tubing, roasting bread dough over campfires, and sporting matching Benetton sweaters. The best.

1. Bring a large pot of salted water to a boil.

2. Meanwhile, in a large frying pan, heat the olive oil and butter over medium-low heat. Add the shallot and cook until translucent and fragrant, about 2 minutes, stirring occasionally. Add the garlic and cook for 30 seconds. Stir in the white wine, increase the heat to medium-high, and cook until the wine is reduced by a third, 3 to 4 minutes.

3. Meanwhile, add the pasta to the boiling water and cook until just tender, 3 to 5 minutes. Reserve 1 cup (250 mL) of the pasta water and drain the pasta.

4. While the pasta is cooking, add the broccoli, mushrooms, carrots, asparagus, and zucchini to the frying pan and cook, stirring, until the vegetables are fork-tender but still bright and colourful, 3 to 5 minutes. Stir in the tomatoes and parsley, then add the cooked pasta and toss with tongs to combine. Add some pasta water if needed to make the pasta loose and velvety.

5. Remove from the heat, add the cheese, and toss again. Season with salt and pepper.

6. Divide the pasta among pasta bowls and garnish with additional parsley and cheese. Serve immediately.

3 tablespoons (45 mL) extra-virgin olive oil

2 tablespoons (30 mL) butter or vegan butter

¼ cup (60 mL) finely chopped shallot (1 medium shallot)

2 large cloves garlic, minced

1 cup (250 mL) dry white wine (we use pinot gris)

⅔ pound (300 g) capellini

1 cup (250 mL) bite-size broccoli florets

1 cup (250 mL) sliced white mushrooms

1 cup (250 mL) finely chopped peeled carrots

1 cup (250 mL) trimmed asparagus cut into ½-inch (1 cm) pieces

1 cup (250 mL) finely chopped zucchini

3 small tomatoes, seeded and chopped

1 cup (250 mL) finely chopped fresh flat-leaf parsley, more for garnish

⅔ cup (150 mL) crumbled feta cheese or grated Parmesan cheese or Vegan Parm (page 314), more for garnish

Salt and pepper

VEGAN: Use vegan butter and Vegan Parm (page 314) or skip the cheese.

GLUTEN-FREE: Use gluten-free pasta.

SQUASH RISOTTO WITH FRIED SAGE

Serves 4 to 6

Risotto is the food equivalent of a hug in a bowl, and this squash risotto takes comfort food to a new level. Roasting the squash brings out its natural sweetness; if you don't feel like dealing with the hassle of peeling the acorn squash (those ridges can be such a pain in the you know what), simply replace it with more butternut squash, which has a sweeter flavour. We love the colour and contrast of using both, but the choice is yours. Risotto takes time to make, so pour yourself a glass of good wine, turn on some chill music, and warm up your stirring arm!

1. Preheat the oven to 400°F (200°C). Line a baking sheet with parchment paper.

2. Place the acorn squash and 1 cup (250 mL) of the butternut squash on the prepared baking sheet, spread it out evenly, and drizzle with ¼ cup (60 mL) of the olive oil. Season with a sprinkle of salt and pepper. Roast until the squash is soft and golden brown on the edges, 45 to 50 minutes. Let cool.

3. Meanwhile, in a medium, heavy-bottomed saucepan, heat 2 tablespoons (30 mL) of the olive oil over medium-low heat. Add 1 cup (250 mL) of the onions and cook until soft and translucent, 3 to 5 minutes, stirring occasionally. Add one clove of crushed garlic and cook, stirring, for 1 minute. Add the remaining 2 cups (500 mL) butternut squash and 2 cups (500 mL) of the vegetable stock and simmer until the squash is very soft, 10 to 15 minutes, stirring occasionally. Remove from the heat and stir in the lemon juice. Purée using an immersion blender or high-speed blender. You may need to add more stock to get a thinner purée. Season with salt and pepper and set aside.

4. In a small frying pan over medium heat, heat 2 tablespoons (30 mL) of the olive oil. Add the sage leaves and cook until they are crispy but not turning brown, 2 to 3 minutes. Using tongs, transfer the fried sage leaves to a plate lined with paper towel and set aside.

5. In a large saucepan, bring the remaining 8 cups (2 L) vegetable stock to a simmer, then reduce the heat to low and cover.

2 pounds (900 g) acorn squash, peeled and cut into ½-inch (1 cm) cubes

3 pounds (1.4 kg) butternut squash, peeled and cut into ½-inch (1 cm) cubes (3 cups/750 mL), divided

¼ cup (60 mL) + 6 tablespoons (90 mL) olive oil, divided

Salt and pepper

3 cups (750 mL) finely chopped yellow onion, divided (1½ large onions)

3 cloves garlic, crushed, divided

10 cups (2.4 L) vegetable stock, divided

1 teaspoon (5 mL) fresh lemon juice

¼ cup (60 mL) fresh sage leaves (about 12 leaves)

2 cups (500 mL) Arborio rice

1 cup (250 mL) white wine (we use pinot gris)

½ cup (125 mL) grated Parmesan cheese or Vegan Parm (page 314), more for serving

Continued . . .

6. In a large, heavy-bottomed pot, heat the remaining 2 tablespoons (30 mL) olive oil over medium-low heat. Add the remaining 2 cups (500 mL) onions and cook until soft and translucent, 3 to 4 minutes, stirring occasionally. Add the remaining 2 cloves crushed garlic and cook, stirring, for 1 minute.

7. Add the rice and cook, stirring constantly, for 3 to 4 minutes to gently toast the rice.

8. Add the white wine and cook, stirring, until the wine is absorbed into the rice. Stir in ½ cup (125 mL) of the hot vegetable stock and cook, stirring, until the stock is absorbed into the rice, about 2 minutes. Repeat, adding ½ cup (125 mL) stock at a time and stirring until each addition has been fully absorbed into the rice and it becomes thick, until the rice is creamy and soft with a slight bite to it, 20 to 25 minutes. You may not use all the stock.

9. Stir in the roasted squash, Parmesan, and salt and pepper to taste.

10. To serve, ladle a few spoonfuls of the squash purée into shallow bowls and spoon the risotto in the centre of the purée. Garnish with additional Parmesan and a few crisp sage leaves and serve immediately.

VEGAN: Use Vegan Parm (page 314).

GLUTEN-FREE: Use gluten-free vegetable stock.

LENTIL SHEPHERD'S PIE

Serves 8

Filled with veggie goodness, this hearty vegetarian version of shepherd's pie will leave your body saying "Thank you!" We love the sweet, earthy flavour and colour that the sweet potato layer gives to the dish. Lentils are a nutrition powerhouse, loaded with plant protein, fibre, folate, and iron. Shepherd's pie is the ideal comfort food to serve on a cool fall evening, and it can be made ahead for easy entertaining. Pull out this recipe to prepare for dinner following afternoons of picking pumpkins and sipping hot apple cider on those crisp fall days.

I. MAKE THE POTATO TOPPING Bring 2 large pots of salted water to a boil. Add the russet potatoes to one pot and the sweet potatoes to the other pot. Cook at a low rolling boil until fork-tender, 15 to 20 minutes. Drain each pot and place the potatoes back in their respective pots (keep them separate).

2. In a small saucepan, heat the vegan butter and Cashew Cream over low heat until the butter is melted.

3. Using a potato masher, mash the russet potatoes and the sweet potatoes in their pots. Add half of the butter mixture to each of the pots and mash each potato mixture until smooth. Season with salt and pepper. Set aside.

4. Preheat the oven to 350°F (180°C).

5. MAKE THE FILLING Heat the olive oil in a large, heavy-bottomed frying pan or pot over medium heat. Add the onion and cook until soft and translucent, 3 to 4 minutes, stirring occasionally.

6. Add the garlic and cook, stirring, until translucent and fragrant, 1 to 2 minutes. Add the white mushrooms, portobello mushrooms, carrots, and celery and cook until the vegetables are softened, about 8 minutes, stirring occasionally.

7. Add the red wine, stir well, and cook until the mixture has reduced by three-quarters. Stir in the lentils, vegetable stock, parsley, and thyme, reduce the heat to medium-low, and cook until the lentils are soft, about 30 minutes, stirring occasionally.

Potato Topping

2 pounds (900 g) russet potatoes, peeled and cut into I-inch (2.5 cm) cubes (about 5 large potatoes)

2 pounds (900 g) sweet potatoes, peeled and cut into I-inch (2.5 cm) cubes (about 5 sweet potatoes)

½ cup (125 mL) vegan butter

½ cup (125 mL) Cashew Cream (page 313)

Salt and pepper

Filling

¼ cup (60 mL) extra-virgin olive oil

2 cups (500 mL) finely chopped sweet onion (I large onion)

2 cloves garlic, crushed

4 cups (I L) sliced white mushrooms (10 ounces/280 g)

2 portobello mushrooms, gills removed, finely chopped

I cup (250 mL) peeled and finely chopped carrots

½ cup (125 mL) finely chopped celery (2 to 3 stalks)

I cup (250 mL) red wine (we use merlot)

I cup (250 mL) green lentils, rinsed

Continued . . .

8. Stir in the ketchup, tamari, peas, and corn. Season with salt and pepper.

9. Spoon the mixture into a 13- × 9-inch (3 L) baking dish and level the top with the back of a large spoon. Spread the sweet potatoes on top of the filling, carefully spreading to the edges with the back of the spoon. Spread the russet potatoes on top, carefully spreading to the edges. You can add texture to the potato layer with the back of a fork prior to baking, if desired.

10. Bake for 30 to 40 minutes, until the filling starts to bubble. Turn the oven to broil and lightly brown the top (watch so it does not burn). Serve hot.

GLUTEN-FREE: Use gluten-free vegetable stock, ketchup, and tamari.

4 to 5 cups (1 to 1.25 L) vegetable stock

¼ cup (60 mL) finely chopped flat-leaf parsley

1 tablespoon (15 mL) fresh thyme leaves

¼ cup (60 mL) ketchup

1 teaspoon (5 mL) tamari

1 cup (250 mL) frozen peas

1 cup (250 mL) frozen corn kernels

Salt and pepper

VEGGIE STEW WITH DUMPLINGS

Serves 4 to 6

Growing up in freezing northern Alberta winters meant coming home to lots of warm one-pot dishes, including stew with dumplings, which remains one of our Granny's favourite meals to make. Of course, our childhood version was *loaded* with beef. We set out to create a veggie stew with all of the richness and heartiness of its meaty counterpart, and we are pretty darn happy with the result, if we say so ourselves! Adding the cold vegan butter at the end really softens the flavour of the stew. The dumplings really expand while cooking, so do not be tempted to make them bigger than the suggested size.

1. MAKE THE VEGGIE STEW Tie the bay leaves, rosemary, and thyme sprigs together tightly with cooking twine and set aside.

2. Heat the olive oil in a medium, heavy-bottomed pot over medium heat. Add the onions and cook until soft and translucent, 3 to 5 minutes, stirring occasionally. Add the garlic and mushrooms and cook, stirring frequently, until the mushrooms are soft, about 5 minutes.

3. Add the red wine, stir well, and cook until the wine is reduced by about half.

4. Add the herb bundle, carrots, potatoes, parsnips, 4 cups (1 L) of the vegetable stock, and tomato paste. Cover and simmer over medium-low heat until the vegetables are fork-tender, 45 to 60 minutes, stirring occasionally and adding more stock if the stew gets too thick.

5. Remove the herb bundle and discard. Season stew with salt and pepper. Stir in the cold vegan butter.

Veggie Stew

2 bay leaves

3 sprigs fresh rosemary

6 sprigs fresh thyme

3 tablespoons (45 mL) extra-virgin olive oil

1½ cups (375 mL) finely chopped yellow onion (1 large onion)

3 cloves garlic, crushed

9 ounces (250 g) quartered white and/or brown mushrooms (about 3 cups /750 mL)

1 cup (250 mL) red wine (we use cabernet sauvignon)

4 carrots, peeled and cut into 2-inch (5 cm) lengths

3 large yellow potatoes, peeled and quartered (about 1 pound/450 g)

2 parsnips, peeled and cut into 2-inch (5 cm) lengths

4 to 5½ cups (1 to 1.25 L) vegetable stock (we use beef-flavoured vegetarian stock)

1 tablespoon (15 mL) tomato paste

Salt and pepper

1 tablespoon (15 mL) cold vegan butter

1 cup (250 mL) frozen peas

Continued . . .

6. MAKE THE DUMPLINGS Combine the almond milk and vegan butter in a small saucepan and simmer over low heat until the butter is melted. Remove from the heat and cool slightly.

7. Meanwhile, whisk together the flour, baking powder, and salt in a medium bowl. Pour the milk mixture into the flour mixture, add the parsley (if using), and stir with a wooden spoon until just combined (it will look rough).

8. Stir the peas into the stew. Using floured hands, pull off golf-ball-sized balls of dough and gently drop them evenly on top of the stew. Cover and simmer until the dumplings are cooked through and have doubled in size, about 10 minutes.

9. Ladle the stew into bowls, top with some dumplings, and serve.

GLUTEN-FREE: Use gluten-free vegetable stock. Skip the dumplings.

NUT-FREE: Use soy milk instead of almond milk.

Dumplings

1¼ cups (300 mL) unsweetened almond milk or soy milk

¼ cup (60 mL) vegan butter

2 cups (500 mL) all-purpose flour

1 tablespoon (15 mL) baking powder

1 teaspoon (5 mL) salt

⅓ cup (75 mL) finely chopped fresh flat-leaf parsley (optional)

VEGGIE POT PIE

Serves 4 to 6

Pot pie is one of our all-time favourite dishes that Tori used to make back in our Vancouver days when the rain was pouring cats and dogs on those lazy Sunday afternoons. Nothing has changed, really. We still live a stone's throw from each other, and Tori still loves to cook this dish. But it has evolved over the years. The original version had chicken in it and was topped with buttery pastry, but we guarantee you will not miss the chicken in this hearty vegetarian version. Tender biscuits top a bubbling, creamy vegetable filling for those nights when all you want is a big cozy blanket and your best friend.

1. Preheat the oven to 425°F (220°C).

2. MAKE THE VEGGIE POT PIE FILLING In a large heavy-bottomed pot, heat the olive oil and vegan butter over medium heat. Add the onions and cook until soft and translucent, 3 to 4 minutes, stirring occasionally. Add the garlic and cook for 30 seconds. Add the celery and mushrooms and cook until the mushrooms are softened, 8 to 10 minutes.

3. Sprinkle the flour over the mixture and cook for 1 minute, stirring constantly. Add the white wine and cook, stirring constantly, 2 to 3 minutes. Add the vegetarian stock, carrots, corn, peas, Cashew Cream, parsley, dill, poultry seasoning, and salt and pepper to taste. Cook until the mixture is slightly thickened, 2 to 4 minutes, stirring occasionally.

4. Pour the filling into an 11- × 7- inch (2 L) baking dish and set aside.

Veggie Pot Pie Filling

3 tablespoons (45 mL) extra-virgin olive oil

3 tablespoons (45 mL) vegan butter

2 cups (500 mL) finely chopped yellow onion (1 large onion)

4 cloves garlic, crushed

1½ cups (375 mL) finely chopped celery (3 stalks)

1 pound (450 g) sliced white mushrooms (about 6 cups/1.5 L)

4 teaspoons (20 mL) all-purpose flour

¾ cup (175 mL) dry white wine (we use chardonnay)

1½ cups (375 ml) chicken-flavoured vegetarian stock (see Tip)

2 cups (500 mL) peeled and finely chopped carrots (2 to 3 large carrots)

1½ cups (375 mL) frozen corn kernels

1½ cups (375 mL) frozen peas

1½ cups (375 mL) Cashew Cream (page 313)

½ cup (125 mL) lightly packed chopped fresh flat-leaf parsley

3 tablespoons (45 mL) chopped fresh dill

½ teaspoon (2 mL) poultry seasoning

Salt and pepper

Continued . . .

5. MAKE THE BISCUIT TOPPING In a large bowl, sift together the flour, baking powder, sugar, and salt. Lightly mix the cold vegan butter into the flour mixture with a pastry blender or your fingers until the pieces are the size of peas. Add the almond milk and stir with a fork in a light tossing motion until just combined (do not overmix the dough).

6. On a lightly floured work surface, shape the dough into a flat disc about ¾ inch (2 cm) thick. Cut out circles with a 3-inch (8 cm) round cookie cutter. You should have at least 6 biscuits, rerolling scraps if necessary.

7. Arrange the biscuits evenly on top of the filling. Brush the top of each biscuit with the melted vegan butter. Bake until the filling is bubbling and the biscuits are lightly browned, 25 to 35 minutes. Spoon into bowls and serve.

Biscuit Topping

2 cups (500 mL) all-purpose flour

4 teaspoons (20 mL) baking powder

1 teaspoon (5 mL) sugar

½ teaspoon (2 mL) salt

½ cup (125 mL) cold vegan butter, cut into ½-inch (1 cm) cubes

¾ cup (175 mL) unsweetened almond milk

2 tablespoons (30 mL) vegan butter, melted

TIP: Use regular vegetable stock if you cannot find chicken-flavoured vegetarian stock.

MUSHROOM WELLINGTON

Makes 2 Wellingtons; serves 10 to 12

Finding plant-based main dishes for a holiday meal like Thanksgiving can be a serious challenge! It turns out that replacing the ham or turkey was trickier than we thought when we first tackled a vegan Thanksgiving. We played around with a few ideas and finally fell head over heels in love with this dish that Jillian created—she seriously knocked it out of the park! This veggie Wellington is packed with goodness, super hearty, and absolutely craveable, and it had *all* of our meat-eating family members begging for more (not an easy thing, for the record). To top it off, the filling can be prepared a day in advance. It is as close to perfect as they come.

1. Preheat the oven to 400°F (200°C). Line a baking sheet with parchment paper.

2. MAKE THE POTATO MIXTURE In a large nonstick frying pan, melt the vegan butter over medium-low heat. Add the potatoes and cook, stirring, until softened, about 5 minutes. Add the carrots and celery and cook, stirring occasionally, until the vegetables are soft, about 10 minutes. Remove from the heat and scrape the mixture into a medium bowl.

3. MAKE THE MUSHROOM MIXTURE In the same frying pan, melt the vegan butter over medium heat. Add the onions and cook until soft and translucent, about 4 minutes, stirring occasionally. Add the garlic and mushrooms and continue to cook, stirring occasionally, until the mushrooms soften, 3 to 5 minutes. Add the concentrated vegetarian stock, red wine, thyme, and sage. Cook until the wine is reduced by half.

4. Add the mushroom mixture to the potato mixture. Stir in the panko crumbs and season with salt and pepper. (The filling can be made 1 day ahead. Keep in the fridge, covered.)

5. ASSEMBLE THE MUSHROOM WELLINGTONS Arrange one sheet of puff pastry on a work surface with the long side facing you. Spoon half of the vegetable mixture lengthwise across the lower-half of the pastry, leaving a 2- to 3-inch (5 to 8 cm) border, pressing the mixture together with your hands to form a roll. Fold the sides of the pastry over the filling, then roll it up, starting at the end closest to you. Repeat with the second Wellington.

Potato Mixture

3 tablespoons (45 mL) vegan butter or extra-virgin olive oil

2 cups (500 mL) peeled and finely chopped white or red potatoes (2 large potatoes)

2 cups (500 mL) peeled and finely chopped carrots (3 to 4 large carrots)

1 cup (250 mL) finely chopped celery (3 to 4 stalks)

Mushroom Mixture

¼ cup (60 mL) vegan butter

2 cups (500 mL) finely chopped yellow onion (1 large onion)

4 cloves garlic, crushed

4 cups (1 L) finely chopped white and/or brown mushrooms (about 1 pound/450 g)

1 tablespoon (15 mL) beef-flavoured concentrated vegetarian stock

½ cup (125 mL) red wine (we use merlot)

2 teaspoons (10 mL) chopped fresh thyme

2 teaspoons (10 mL) finely chopped fresh sage

1½ cups (375 mL) panko crumbs

Salt and pepper

Continued . . .

6. Place the Wellingtons on the prepared baking sheet, leaving space between them. Lightly brush the Wellingtons with the melted vegan butter. Bake until golden brown, 25 to 30 minutes.

7. Transfer the Wellingtons to a long plate or a platter and garnish with the fresh thyme sprigs. To serve, cut into thick slices using a large, sharp knife.

For assembly

2 sheets (10- × 15-inches/ 25 × 38 cm each) vegan puff pastry, thawed (from a block of puff pastry)

2 tablespoons (30 mL) melted vegan butter or extra-virgin olive oil

4 to 6 sprigs fresh thyme, for garnish

TOFU FRIED RICE

Serves 4

Growing up in Peace River, in northern Alberta, there were not exactly a ton of restaurants to choose from. We remember when the town got its first set of traffic lights, if that says anything! But by some stroke of luck we ended up with a killer Chinese restaurant called the Golden Palace where, as kids, we used to order virgin chi chis with fancy umbrellas and feel all special when Frank, the owner, would come out and see us. Golden Palace was such a big deal to us that when Tori and her brother Terry moved to Kelowna, Terry used to cry, "I miss Frank's chicken balls." This veggie-heavy fried rice is hearty enough to be a main course thanks to the addition of the tofu. We think Frank would approve.

1. PREPARE THE TOFU Press the tofu by placing it between 2 sheets of paper towel, then sandwich it between 2 plates. Place a heavy object such as another plate weighted with bags of beans on top; let sit at room temperature for at least 1 hour or overnight, covered, in the fridge.

2. Cut the tofu into ½-inch (1 cm) cubes and squeeze them into a small, shallow container (the tofu should be cozy in there so the marinade covers all of it).

3. In a small bowl, whisk together the soy sauce, rice wine vinegar, brown sugar, sesame oil, and garlic. Pour the marinade over the tofu, cover the container, and let sit for 2 to 4 hours. (If you are in a hurry, microwave the tofu in the marinade for 1 to 2 minutes and then let it cool for 15 minutes.)

4. Heat the peanut oil in a large frying pan over medium heat. Drain the tofu cubes (discard the marinade) and fry until crispy on all sides. Transfer to a plate and set aside. Set aside the frying pan.

5. MAKE THE FRIED RICE Cook the rice until tender according to the package directions (the cooking time will depend on the type of rice you use). Once cooked, transfer the rice to a baking sheet lined with parchment paper, spread it out and set it aside to cool.

6. Once the rice has cooled, heat 1 tablespoon (15 mL) of the peanut oil in the frying pan over medium heat. Add the onion and cook, stirring occasionally, until soft and translucent, 3 to 5 minutes. Add the garlic and cook, stirring, for 1 minute.

Tofu

1 package (12 ounces/350 g) extra-firm tofu, drained

⅓ cup (75 mL) soy sauce

¼ cup (60 mL) rice wine vinegar

1 tablespoon (15 mL) firmly packed brown sugar

1 tablespoon (15 mL) sesame oil

3 cloves garlic, crushed

1 tablespoon (15 mL) peanut oil

Fried Rice

1½ cups (375 mL) long-grain white or brown rice (makes 4 cups/1 L cooked rice)

3 tablespoons (45 mL) peanut oil, divided

½ cup (125 mL) finely chopped yellow onion

2 cloves garlic, crushed

1 heaping tablespoon (18 mL) grated fresh ginger

1 cup (250 mL) diced peeled carrots

1 cup (250 mL) sliced brown and/or white mushrooms

1 cup (250 mL) diced celery

2 tablespoons (30 mL) soy sauce

1 cup (250 mL) fresh or frozen peas

1 to 2 green onions (white and light green parts only), sliced, for garnish

Continued . . .

7. Add the ginger, carrots, and mushrooms and continue to cook, stirring occasionally, until the mushrooms just start to soften (you do not want them to brown), 3 to 5 minutes.

8. Add the celery and cook until it is slightly cooked but still crisp, 1 to 2 minutes. Transfer the vegetable mixture to a medium bowl and set aside.

9. Heat the remaining 2 tablespoons (30 mL) peanut oil in the frying pan over medium-high heat. Add the rice and cook, stirring occasionally, until it just starts to brown. Add the soy sauce, peas, cooked vegetables, and crispy tofu. Cook, stirring, until the peas are cooked but still bright green, 3 to 4 minutes.

10. Transfer the Tofu Fried Rice to a large serving bowl, garnish with sliced green onion, and serve.

GLUTEN-FREE: Use gluten-free soy sauce.

NUT-FREE: Substitute vegetable oil for the peanut oil.

GRANNY'S OVERHAULED BAKED BEANS

Serves 6 to 8

Our granny makes *the best* baked beans we have ever eaten. It only occurred to us recently to get the recipe from her—I guess we just always relied on Granny to make them! Many baked bean recipes call for molasses and a heap of other ingredients, but hers are simple and honest. Of course, they're also loaded with bacon. *Many* batches of baked beans later, we figured out a way to make them vegan with a gluten-free option (see below) while maintaining the simplicity of Granny's recipe. Baking the beans at the end may seem like an unnecessary step since the beans are already cooked but it really intensifies the flavour of the beans. Serve our Granny-approved beans with Molasses Oatmeal Bread (page 233) or a batch of Perfect White Buns (page 239) and you will have one happy crowd. This is an awesome and easy meal to make ahead for effortless entertaining on a cozy fall or winter night.

4 cups (1 L) dried navy beans

¼ cup (60 mL) extra-virgin olive oil

4 cups (1 L) finely chopped yellow onions (2 large onions)

4 cups (1 L) gluten-free prepared tomato soup or 2 cans (10 ounces/284 mL each) condensed tomato soup

⅓ cup (75 mL) firmly packed brown sugar or pure maple syrup

1 to 2 teaspoons (5 to 10 mL) salt

3 drops hickory liquid smoke, more as needed

1. Rinse the navy beans in a colander and place them in a large stock pot. Cover the beans with 2 inches (5 cm) of water, bring to a boil, then remove from the heat and let sit, uncovered, for 1 hour.

2. Drain the beans and put them back in the pot. Cover them with 2 inches (5 cm) of fresh water again and bring to a simmer. Cover with a lid and cook the beans, stirring occasionally, until tender and slightly split, about 2 hours. The water level should go down to below the top of the beans during cooking; add just enough water, if needed, to keep the beans from burning.

3. Meanwhile, in a large frying pan, heat the olive oil over medium-low heat. Add the onions, reduce the heat to low, and cook, stirring occasionally, until the onions are light golden brown, 20 to 30 minutes. Remove from the heat.

4. When the beans are fully cooked, add the cooked onions, tomato soup, brown sugar, salt to taste, and hickory liquid smoke to taste. Stir to mix, and cook over medium-low heat for a further 20 minutes, stirring occasionally.

5. Meanwhile, preheat the oven to 300°F (150°C).

6. Transfer the beans to a baking dish with a lid or a bean pot, cover, and bake for about 3 hours, stirring occasionally.

GLUTEN-FREE: Use gluten-free tomato soup and skip the hickory smoke.

VEGETARIAN CHILI

Serves 8 to 10

Jillian's dad, Glen, is basically superman. He cleans, he can fix anything, he is funny (hilarious, actually), and he cooks! He was sweet enough to write out his chili recipe to share in this cookbook, so here it is. Okay, with maybe a few tweaks, such as minus the beef. Sorry, Dad! Like many one-pot meals, this chili tastes even better the next day. Serve it with our Skillet Cornbread (page 231) or steamed white or brown rice.

1. Heat the olive oil and vegan butter in a large, heavy-bottomed pot over medium-low heat. Add the onions and cook until soft and translucent, 3 to 4 minutes, stirring occasionally. Add the garlic, celery, portobello mushrooms, and white mushrooms and continue to cook until the mushrooms are soft, about 10 minutes, stirring occasionally.

2. Stir in the stock concentrate, potatoes, tomatoes with their juice, corn, baked beans, kidney beans, chili powder, oregano, and sugar. Reduce the heat to low and cook, uncovered, until the potatoes are fork-tender, 45 to 60 minutes. Season with salt and pepper.

GLUTEN-FREE: Use gluten-free stock concentrate and baked beans.

¼ cup (60 mL) extra-virgin olive oil

2 tablespoons (30 mL) vegan butter

I medium yellow onion, finely chopped

3 cloves garlic, crushed

3 stalks celery, finely chopped

2 portobello mushrooms, gills removed, chopped

12 ounces (340 g) sliced white and/or brown mushrooms (about 4 cups/I L)

I tablespoon (15 mL) beef-flavoured vegetarian stock concentrate

2 cups (500 mL) peeled white or red potatoes cut into ½-inch (I cm) cubes (2 to 3 medium potatoes)

I can (28 ounces/796 mL) diced tomatoes

1½ cups (375 mL) frozen corn kernels

I can (14 ounces/398 mL) vegetarian baked beans

I can (19 ounces/540 mL) kidney beans, drained and rinsed

2 to 4 tablespoons (3(to 60 mL) chili powder

I teaspoon (5 mL) dried oregano

I teaspoon (5 mL) sugar

Salt and pepper

BARBECUE VEGAN JACKFRUIT "PULLED PORK" SLIDERS

Serves 4

When Jillian started going plant-based, she missed pork the most. In fact, she could not get pulled pork out of her head. She tried a few vegan versions, and although they were good, they were *too healthy* and missing the salt and fat of the original. All to say that this recipe might not necessarily be the healthiest recipe ever, but Wilbur was saved! Even the meat-lovers in our family love it. Plus, it's way easier to make than traditional pulled pork, so you will thank Jillian later. Yum!

1. MAKE THE JACKFRUIT "PULLED PORK" SLIDERS Preheat the oven to 350°F (180°C). Line a baking sheet with parchment paper.

2. Heat the olive oil in a large frying pan over medium heat. Add the onions and cook until just turning golden brown, 4 to 5 minutes, stirring occasionally. Add the garlic and cook, stirring, for 1 minute. Add the jackfruit and cook until golden brown, 4 to 5 minutes per side.

3. Transfer the jackfruit to a large bowl. Add the barbecue sauce, melted vegan butter, water, and stock concentrate. Toss to combine.

4. Spread the jackfruit on the prepared baking sheet and bake for 1 hour, stirring occasionally and adding 1 to 2 tablespoons (15 to 30 mL) water if it dries out (it's okay if the edges get a bit crispy; it adds to the texture).

5. Remove from the oven and, using 2 forks, pull the jackfruit apart to shred it. Return to the oven and bake for an additional 20 to 30 minutes, until the jackfruit is crispy on the edges.

6. MEANWHILE, MAKE THE COLESLAW In a medium bowl, combine the vegan mayonnaise, lime juice, sugar, cider vinegar, and salt; stir well. Add the cabbage, carrots, and cilantro and toss to combine. Cover and refrigerate until ready to use.

7. ASSEMBLE THE SLIDERS Butter the buns and toast in a frying pan. Place a generous serving (about ½ cup/125 mL) of the baked jackfruit on the bottom half of each bun. Top with a scoop of Coleslaw, a generous spoonful of Pineapple Salsa, and a couple of slices of avocado and serve.

GLUTEN-FREE: Use gluten-free barbecue sauce, stock concentrate, and mayonnaise, and serve on a gluten-free bun.

Jackfruit "Pulled Pork" Sliders

2 tablespoons (30 mL) extra-virgin olive oil

1½ cups (375 mL) finely chopped yellow onions (1 medium onion)

2 cloves garlic, crushed

2 cans (20 ounces/567 g each) green jackfruit in brine, well drained

1¼ cups (300 mL) barbecue sauce

⅓ cup (75 mL) vegan butter, melted

¼ cup (60 mL) water

1 teaspoon (5 mL) beef-flavoured vegetarian stock concentrate

Coleslaw

⅓ cup (75 mL) vegan mayonnaise

Juice of 1 lime

2 teaspoons (10 mL) sugar

1½ teaspoons (7 mL) apple cider vinegar

¼ teaspoon (1 mL) salt

3 cups (750 mL) shredded or thinly sliced red cabbage (use a mandoline)

1¼ cups (300 mL) peeled and shredded carrot

¾ cup (175 mL) chopped fresh cilantro

For serving

Vegan butter

4 crusty buns

Pineapple Salsa (page 113)

Sliced avocado

SEAFOOD "BAKE"

Serves 4

Doing a seafood bake (or grill, as that's what this recipe really is) is such a fun way to entertain. Pull out the bibs and the napkins—you're going to need them! The key to this recipe is a grill basket: we recommend buying two of them so that you can grill all the ingredients at once. Be careful to not overcook the shellfish, or it will be dry. This recipe is perfect on its own and so flavourful, but you can take the meal to the next level by serving Cheddar Chive Biscuits (page 235) instead of the baguette. Serve in an oversized serving dish or directly on a table you have lined with newspaper or brown paper.

1. MAKE THE MARINADE Melt the butter and garlic in a small saucepan over low heat until the butter just starts to bubble (do not let it brown). Stir in the white wine, Old Bay seasoning, and thyme and simmer for 2 to 3 minutes. Season with salt, to taste. Set aside and cool to room temperature.

2. MAKE THE SEAFOOD GRILL Bring a large pot of well-salted water to a boil. Boil the baby potatoes until they are fork-tender but still a bit firm (the cooking time will depend on the size of the potatoes). Transfer the potatoes to a colander using a slotted spoon, then place them in a large bowl and set aside.

3. Cook the corn in the same water until tender, about 10 minutes. Transfer to a colander with tongs and rinse under cold water to stop the cooking. Once cool enough to touch, cut the cobs into 2- to 3-inch (5 to 8 cm) pieces. Set aside.

4. Once the marinade is cool (you should be able to hold your finger in it comfortably, otherwise it will cook the seafood), place the potatoes, corn, clams, mussels, prawns, and prepared lobster in a large resealable plastic bag. Add ¾ cup (175 mL) of the marinade (reserve the remaining marinade). Seal the bag and turn and massage it a bit to ensure the marinade completely coats everything.

5. Preheat a grill for direct cooking over medium-high heat.

Marinade

1 cup (250 mL) butter or vegan butter

3 cloves garlic, crushed

⅓ cup (75 mL) white wine (we use sauvignon blanc)

1 tablespoon + 2 teaspoons (25 mL) Old Bay seasoning

4 sprigs fresh thyme

Salt

Seafood Grill

2 pounds (900 g) baby white or red potatoes

3 corn cobs, husked

1 pound (450 g) fresh clams, scrubbed

1 pound (450 g) fresh mussels, scrubbed and beards removed

½ pound (225 g) large fresh prawns, unpeeled

2 fresh lobsters, halved lengthwise, claws separated (ask your fishmonger to kill and clean the lobsters if cooking immediately, or see page 190 for instructions)

2 lemons, cut in half

1 baguette

Extra-virgin olive oil

Continued . . .

6. Place the seafood in one grill basket and the marinated vegetables in the second grill basket. Place the baskets on the grill, close the cover, and grill until the clams and mussels open up and the lobster is firm and opaque, 6 to 8 minutes. Remove the baskets from the grill. Discard any clams or mussels that did not open.

7. Using tongs, place the corn and the lemon halves (cut side down) directly on the grill for 2 to 4 minutes, until grill marks appear. Transfer the corn along with the grilled seafood and vegetables into a large bowl and toss everything with the reserved marinade.

8. Slice the baguette in half lengthwise and brush the cut sides with olive oil. Grill the baguette cut side down until grill marks appear.

9. Serve immediately with tons of napkins, the grilled baguette and lemon halves, and crisp white wine in tumblers.

DAIRY-FREE: Use vegan butter.

How to Prepare a Lobster for Grilling

If your lobster is alive, place it in the freezer for 20 minutes.

Place the lobster on its back on a cutting board. Using a large, sharp knife, make a quick lengthwise incision in the area between its legs and claws, and then follow through by bringing the knife down, dividing the head.

With the lobster still on its back, split it into two halves lengthwise by slicing from its head to its tail. Remove any tomalley or eggs (reserving them, if you like). Break off both claws.

SALMON SPANAKOPITAS WITH DILL TZATZIKI

Serves 6 to 8

These tasty filo bundles take a bit of time to prepare, but they are bursting with Greek flavours and so impressive—a real showstopper for weekend entertaining! The spinach and herb filling is a perfect complement to the salmon, and even better, can be prepared in advance. Our Dill Tzatziki is superior to anything you can buy, but feel free to use premade if you do not feel like the extra work.

1. MAKE THE DILL TZATZIKI Place the grated cucumber in a fine sieve placed over a small bowl, mix in the salt, and let sit for about 45 minutes, periodically pressing down on the cucumber and turning it over to remove as much moisture as possible.

2. In a medium bowl, stir together the yogurt, lemon juice, dill, olive oil, and garlic. Stir in the cucumber and refrigerate until ready to use.

3. MAKE THE SALMON SPANAKOPITAS Pat the salmon fillets dry with paper towel and set aside at room temperature.

4. In a medium frying pan, heat the olive oil over medium heat. Add the onion and cook until translucent, 3 to 4 minutes, stirring occasionally. Add the green onions and garlic and cook, stirring, for 1 minute. Remove from the heat.

5. Using a paper towel or a kitchen towel, squeeze any excess liquid out of the spinach (any excess will make the phyllo pastry soggy). Place the drained spinach in a medium bowl and add the cooked onion mixture, feta, parsley, dill, oregano, and lemon zest. Mix together thoroughly—you may find it easier to use your hands. Season with salt and pepper and stir in the egg, mixing thoroughly.

6. Preheat the oven to 425°F (220°C). Line a baking sheet with parchment paper.

7. Remove the phyllo from the box, keeping it on the paper, and cover with plastic wrap and a slightly damp kitchen towel to keep it from drying out.

8. Season the salmon fillets with salt.

Dill Tzatziki

1 cup (250 mL) grated English cucumber (½ cucumber)

1 teaspoon (5 mL) salt

1 cup (250 mL) plain 2% Greek yogurt

2 tablespoons (30 mL) fresh lemon juice (from 1 lemon)

1 tablespoon (15 mL) chopped fresh dill

1 tablespoon (15 mL) extra-virgin olive oil

1 clove garlic, crushed

Salmon Spanakopitas

6 to 8 skinless wild salmon fillets (4 to 5 ounces/ 115 to 140 g each), at room temperature

2 tablespoons (30 mL) extra-virgin olive oil

1 cup (250 mL) finely chopped sweet onion (1 medium onion)

½ cup (125 mL) chopped green onions (white and light green parts only; about 3 green onions)

2 cloves garlic, crushed

1 package (10½ ounces/300 g) frozen chopped spinach, thawed and well drained

1½ cups (375 mL) crumbled feta cheese

Continued . . .

9. To assemble, place 1 sheet of phyllo on a work surface with the long side facing you, brush it with olive oil, and place another sheet of phyllo directly on top of it, lining up the edges as much as possible (it does not have to be perfect!). Brush with olive oil and place another sheet of phyllo on top.

10. Using a sharp knife, cut the prepared phyllo in half crosswise. Place a salmon fillet at the short end of the pastry. Top with 1 to 2 tablespoons (15 to 30 mL) of the spinach mixture, spreading it evenly on top of the salmon. Starting at the salmon end, roll up the salmon in the phyllo, then fold in the ends. Place seam side down on the prepared baking sheet and repeat with the rest of the salmon fillets. (You will not use all the phyllo.)

11. Lightly brush each spanakopita with olive oil. Bake until golden brown, 12 to 14 minutes. Serve immediately with a dollop of Dill Tzatziki.

DAIRY-FREE: Use dairy-free yogurt to make the Dill Tzatziki. Use Vegan Feta (page 316 or store-bought) in the spinach mixture.

½ cup (125 mL) finely chopped fresh flat-leaf parsley

2 tablespoons (30 mL) chopped fresh dill

1 teaspoon (5 mL) dried oregano

1 teaspoon (5 mL) grated fresh lemon zest

Salt and pepper

1 egg, well beaten

1 package (16 ounces/454 g) phyllo pastry, thawed

Extra-virgin olive oil, for brushing

a

b

c

d

CEDAR-PLANK SALMON BURGERS

Makes 4 burgers

Infused with a perfect hint of smoky flavour from the cedar plank, served on a fresh crusty bun, and topped with a generous scoop of homemade tartar sauce, piles of arugula, and thick slices of garden-fresh tomatoes, these blow any meat burger out of the water! Serve these for your next summer barbeque with extra napkins and some crisp white wine. We make a brine for the salmon to keep it nice and moist. Buy the best wild salmon you can get your hands on—it will really make a difference.

1. At least 2 hours before cooking the salmon, soak the cedar plank in cold water. (We usually do this in the kitchen sink or another large, shallow vessel that will accommodate the plank and weigh it down with something heavy.)

2. In a large bowl, combine the water, sugar, and salt; whisk until the sugar and salt are dissolved. Place the salmon in a large, shallow container (a 13- × 9-inch/3 L pan works well). Pour the brine over the salmon, cover with plastic wrap, and refrigerate for 1 hour.

3. Remove the salmon from the brine, rinse the fillets under cold water, and pat them dry with paper towel. Place the salmon on a plate and let sit at room temperature for 30 minutes.

4. Meanwhile, preheat a grill to high heat.

5. Place the plank on the grill and reduce the heat to medium. Close the lid and allow the plank to heat up until it smokes, about 5 minutes. You may need to adjust the heat setting on your grill depending how hot it gets. Have a squirt bottle with water in it in case the plank flares up.

6. Place the salmon fillets evenly along the plank. Close the lid and cook the fillets 7 to 10 minutes, until just done. They should be just cooked through and lightly browned at the edges, with an internal temperature of 135°F (57°C). The cooking time will vary depending on the thickness of the fillets. Spray the edges of the plank with water if it flares up or move it to a cooler part of the grill. Transfer the cooked fillets to a platter.

7. To assemble, on each bun layer a salmon fillet, desired toppings, and a dollop of Dill Tartar Sauce.

1 untreated cedar plank (we use a 17- × 7-inch/43 × 18 cm plank)

4 cups (1 L) water

2 teaspoons (10 mL) sugar

1 teaspoon (5 mL) salt

4 skinless wild salmon fillets (4 to 5 ounces/115 to 140 g each; we suggest coho, chinook, or sockeye)

For serving

4 kaiser rolls (preferably whole grain)

3 cups (750 mL) loosely packed baby arugula or 8 leaves butter lettuce (optional)

2 large perfectly ripe tomatoes, thinly sliced (optional)

½ medium red onion, thinly sliced (optional)

1 batch of Dill Tartar Sauce (page 121)

POTATO-CRUSTED HALIBUT

Serves 4

In our single days when we lived in Vancouver, we regularly hung our hats at Rodney's Oyster Bar. Countless nights were spent sitting at the bar flirting with the servers as they shucked oysters, drinking grassy Sauvignon Blanc out of tumblers and giggling till we shut the place down. We always ordered the potato-crusted halibut to share, so of course had to replicate it in this book. Halibut meets a potato latke in this dish that is finished with a generous spoonful of homemade dill tartar sauce, taking us right back to the good old days. Make sure you buy fish that is no thicker than about ¾ inch (2 cm). You can substitute any firm white fish for the halibut.

1½ pounds (675 g) russet potatoes, peeled (3 large potatoes)

1½ teaspoons (7 mL) salt, divided

2 eggs

1 cup (250 mL) all-purpose flour

½ teaspoon (2 mL) pepper

4 skinless halibut fillets (4 ounces/115 g each; no more than ¾ inch/2 cm thick), at room temperature

Avocado oil or vegetable oil, for frying

For serving

Dill Tartar Sauce (page 121)

Fresh dill sprigs (optional)

4 lemon wedges

1. Grate the potatoes on the large holes of a box grater or in a food processor using the medium shredding blade. You should have 3 cups (750 mL) of grated potatoes. Place them in a fine sieve set over a bowl, toss with 1 teaspoon (5 mL) of the salt, and set aside for 1 hour, pressing down on them every 20 minutes or so to release as much moisture as possible (they will turn a bit brown—this is okay).

2. Wrap the potatoes in a kitchen towel and wring them over a sink to get rid of any remaining moisture.

3. Beat the eggs in a shallow bowl. Place the flour in a shallow dish and season with pepper and the remaining ½ teaspoon (2 mL) salt.

4. Season the halibut fillets with salt and pepper. Dredge the fillets in the flour, shake off any excess, and dip the fillets in the egg, turning to coat them on all sides. Press a thin layer of grated potato evenly on the top of the fillets (leave the sides uncovered).

5. Heat ¼ inch (5 mm) of avocado oil in a large frying pan over medium heat. Using a metal spatula, carefully transfer the fillets to the pan potato side down. While the fillets are cooking, press another layer of grated potato on the exposed side of the fillets.

6. Cook the fish until golden brown on the bottom, about 5 minutes. Carefully turn and cook for another 3 to 5 minutes, until golden brown on the bottom.

7. Serve the halibut immediately with a generous dollop of Dill Tartar Sauce, garnished with a sprig of fresh dill (if using) and a wedge of lemon.

TORI'S THIN CRUST PIZZA

Makes 6 to 8 pizzas

Nothing beats pizza night! Bust out the Dean Martin, pour a glass of wine, put on your apron, and crank up the oven. Homemade pizza has to be the perfect food for casual entertaining and Tori and Charles' most requested meal. Set out all your toppings in bowls so guests can dig in and create their own pizzas. It makes for an unplugged, fun and relaxed evening that our guests always love: our favourite way to cook! Tori's pizza dough has evolved over the years to embrace a no-knead method that seems like cheating in the baking world but truly makes the *best* pizza dough that will leave you feeling like you just stepped into the streets of Rome. Note that you need to start making the dough the night before. There are a few tricks to mastering pizza: get your oven as hot as you can, invest in a pizza stone, stretch your dough out by hand, not with a rolling pin, and don't overload the pizza with top-pings—a thin-crust pizza does best with a light load.

1. MAKE THE PIZZA DOUGH Whisk together the all-purpose flour, salt, and yeast in a large bowl. Stir in the water with a wooden spoon until well combined, using your hands if needed to work in all the flour. Cover the bowl tightly with plastic wrap and let sit at room temperature for 18 to 20 hours. The dough should double in size.

2. MAKE THE TOMATO SAUCE In a medium, deep bowl, blend the tomatoes with their juice, the basil, oregano, and salt with an immersion blender. Set aside.

3. ASSEMBLE THE PIZZAS Place a pizza stone on the top shelf of the oven and preheat to the highest setting. Let the stone heat for an additional 20 minutes after the oven has reached its set temperature. (If you do not have a pizza stone, you can use a rimless or upside-down baking sheet.)

4. Gently deflate the dough by pushing it down with your hands. Generously sprinkle a work surface with semolina flour, scape the dough onto it, and divide the dough into 6 to 8 equal portions and shape them into balls.

Pizza Dough

5½ cups (1.3 L) all-purpose flour, plus extra for dusting

1 (15 mL) tablespoon salt

½ (2 mL) teaspoon active dry yeast

2½ cups (625 mL) water, at room temperature

Semolina flour, for dusting

Tomato Sauce

1 can (28 ounces/796 mL) good-quality whole Italian tomatoes (we use San Marzano)

¼ cup (60 mL) fresh basil leaves

1 teaspoon (5 mL) dried oregano

1 teaspoon (5 mL) sea salt

Toppings

See page 202 for our favourite combinations

Continued . . .

5. Dust 1 ball of dough with more all-purpose flour. Using your hands, stretch out the dough into a circle that is about 12 inches (30 cm) in diameter. It doesn't have to be perfect or exact, the more rustic the better!

6. Generously sprinkle semolina flour on a pizza peel if you have one (if you don't, simply use a rimless baking sheet). Place the prepared pizza dough on the peel or baking sheet and evenly spread a thin layer of the Tomato Sauce over the dough, stopping about ½ inch (1 cm) from the edge. Scatter the toppings of choice on the pizza, being careful not to overload it, and finish with a small handful of grated cheese (if using). Repeat with the remaining pizzas.

7. To transfer the pizza to the stone, place the peel over the stone and quickly pull the peel back towards you. (Or lift out the hot baking sheet, slide the pizza onto it, and return to the oven.) Bake until the crust is golden brown and the cheese bubbles, 7 to 9 minutes.

8. Use the pizza peel to transfer the pizzas to a large cutting board. Cut into wedges and serve.

VEGAN: Use vegan cheese and toppings.

Favourite Topping Combinations

- Olive oil, mushrooms, thyme, goat cheese or asiago cheese (no tomato sauce) (Tori's favourite)
- Sliced mushrooms, and, after baking, top with fresh arugula tossed in a drizzle of olive oil, squeeze of lemon, and salt and pepper (no cheese) (Jill's favourite)
- Vegan mozzarella cheese, fresh tomatoes, fresh basil
- Veggie ham, vegan mozzarella cheese, red onion, pineapple, fresh cilantro
- Red onion, spicy sausage or vegan Italian sausage, mushrooms, fresh tomatoes, feta cheese
- Grilled firm asparagus, red onion, goat cheese
- Pesto, chicken, red onion, mozzarella
- Olive oil, sliced pear, thyme, Brie, finish with a drizzle of honey after baking (no tomato sauce)
- Green peppers, olives, sweet onion, fresh tomatoes, hot pickled peppers

BIG BURRITOS

Serves 4 to 6

Tacos and burritos rank right up there among our all-time favourite meals. With so much flavour and different healthy fillings to choose from, they are the perfect meal for casual entertaining. This is a great recipe to try as a totally vegan meal if you are new to eating a plant-based diet. One of our meat-loving friends said this was the best burrito he had *ever* eaten! Yahoo! We recommend preparing your fillings and sauces ahead of time and cooking your tempeh just before serving to give you more time for socializing over margaritas (like our Grapefruit Jalapeño Margarita on page 302). The taco seasoning makes more than you'll need; store the extra in an airtight container for up to 6 months. You can also make the Chipotle Sauce ahead of time and freeze it, or freeze extras, for up to 1 month.

Tempeh is made from pressed fermented soy beans and is super healthy and meaty in texture. It can be found near the tofu in most specialty or natural-health grocery stores.

1. MAKE THE TACO SEASONING In a small bowl, stir together the chili powder, salt, cornstarch, cumin, paprika, garlic powder, and oregano. Store in an airtight container for up to 2 months.

2. MAKE THE CHIPOTLE SAUCE In a small frying pan, heat the olive oil over medium-low heat. Add the onion and garlic and cook until the onion starts to soften and turn translucent, about 5 minutes, stirring occasionally.

3. Add the tomatoes, chipotle peppers, sugar, salt, and water. Reduce the heat to low, cover, and cook for 30 to 40 minutes, stirring occasionally. You may need to add a few more tablespoons of water if the sauce starts to get too thick.

4. Transfer the sauce to a deep, narrow bowl and blend with an immersion blender until smooth (be careful not to let it burn you). Transfer to a small serving dish and set aside.

Taco Seasoning (makes about ¾ cup/175 mL)

¼ cup (60 mL) Mexican chili powder

2 tablespoons (30 mL) sea salt

1 tablespoon (15 mL) cornstarch

1 tablespoon (15 mL) ground cumin

1 tablespoon (15 mL) sweet paprika

2 teaspoons (10 mL) garlic powder

2 teaspoons (10 mL) dried oregano

Chipotle Sauce

1 tablespoon (15 mL) extra-virgin olive oil

1 sweet onion, roughly chopped

2 cloves garlic, smashed

4 small tomatoes, roughly chopped

1 to 2 chipotle peppers in adobo sauce

1 teaspoon (5 mL) sugar

½ teaspoon (2 mL) sea salt

¼ cup (60 mL) water

Continued . . .

5. MAKE THE TEMPEH FILLING Heat the olive oil in a medium frying pan over medium heat. Add the crumbled tempeh and cook, stirring occasionally, until browned, 7 to 8 minutes. Reduce the heat to low, add the Taco Seasoning and water, and stir to combine. Simmer until the water has nearly completely evaporated, about 10 minutes. Remove from the heat, cover, and set aside.

6. ASSEMBLE THE BURRITOS Warm the tortillas either by rinsing them under water and heating in a frying pan over medium-low heat for 30 seconds on each side, or wrap the tortillas in foil and place in a 350°F (180°C) oven for 10 to 15 minutes.

7. Lay a softened tortilla on a work surface. In the lower-middle of the tortilla, place a scoop of Tempeh Filling. Add fillings as desired, and top with a spoonful of Chipotle Sauce. Fold the edge closest to you over the filling, tightly roll the burrito half a turn, tuck in both sides (or one if you overfilled it like we always do), and then roll it up completely. Repeat with filling and rolling the remaining burritos. Serve with lime wedges.

VEGAN: Use vegan burrito fillings.

GLUTEN-FREE: Use gluten-free tortillas and ensure that all spices, cheeses, and other ingredients are gluten-free.

NUT-FREE: Use a nut-free sour cream.

Tempeh Filling

2 tablespoons (30 mL) extra-virgin olive oil

2 packages (8 ounces/225 g each) tempeh, crumbled

3 tablespoons (45 mL) Taco Seasoning (recipe on page 203)

1 cup (250 mL) water

4 to 6 large tortillas, warmed (any type, but not small corn tortillas)

Lime wedges, for serving

Fillings (optional)

Canned black beans, warmed

Shredded lettuce

Diced tomatoes

Shredded cheddar cheese, Monterey Jack cheese, or a vegan version

Sour cream, Vegan Sour Cream (page 315), or Cashew Cream (page 313)

Roughly chopped fresh cilantro

Seeded and finely chopped jalapeño pepper

Fresh Salsa (page 118)

Guacamole (page 118)

VEGGIES
& SIDES

POTATO GARLIC CAULIFLOWER MASH

Serves 8

You can always serve regular mashed potatoes, but we prefer our healthier version that packs more nutrition and flavour. We love the rich, cheesy taste of this side dish and tend to add the max amount of ground pepper to ours. The kids love this one! We serve it all year and it is always a hit, zero need to save it for the holiday table. This is a great side dish for the Mushroom Wellington (page 177) along with the Garlicky Greens (page 214) for a hearty but healthy plant-based meal.

1. Place the potatoes, cauliflower, and garlic in a large pot of salted water (enough to cover the veggies) and bring to a boil. Reduce the heat and simmer until the potatoes are fork-tender.

2. Drain the vegetables in a colander, return them to the pot, add the salt and pepper, and mash with a potato masher. Add the vegan butter, nutritional yeast, and ¼ cup (60 mL) of the Cashew Cream and stir until combined. Add more Cashew Cream if needed for desired consistency. Season with more salt and pepper, if desired, and serve.

3 pounds (1.4 kg) large russet potatoes, peeled and quartered (about 5 large potatoes)

1 medium head cauliflower (about 2 pounds/900 g), cored and cut into large chunks

3 cloves garlic

½ teaspoon (2 mL) salt

¼ to ½ teaspoon (1 to 2 mL) pepper

½ cup (125 mL) vegan butter, melted

¼ cup (60 mL) nutritional yeast

¼ to ⅓ cup (60 to 75 mL) Cashew Cream (page 313)

CRISPY ROASTED ROSEMARY POTATOES

Serves 6 to 8

The key to crispy oven-roasted potatoes is to not crowd the pan and not skimp on the olive oil. But the best-kept secret is to shake the daylights out of the potatoes once they are parboiled to loosen up the starch on the outside of the taters. These potatoes have a perfect salty rosemary crispy exterior yet are soft on the inside. Truly perfect! Try making them as an upgrade to your regular hash browns. We like them for breakfast the best: try them with the Tofu Veggie Scramble (page 73) or West Coast Eggs Benny (page 69) to impress your crew!

3 pounds (1.4 kg) yellow potatoes (about 8 medium potatoes)

Salt and pepper

6 tablespoons (90 mL) olive oil

3 tablespoons (45 mL) chopped fresh rosemary

2 or 3 sprigs fresh rosemary and thyme, for garnish

1. Preheat the oven to 450°F (230°C). Line a baking sheet with parchment paper.

2. Wash the potatoes and remove any blemishes, but leave the skin on. Roughly chop the potatoes into 1-inch (2.5 cm) cubes. Place in a large pot, fill with water to cover, and add 1 teaspoon (5 mL) salt. Bring to a boil and cook for 10 to 12 minutes, until the potatoes are just slightly cooked. Drain well in a colander, return them to the pot, and shake them vigorously to roughen up the outside of the potatoes.

3. Turn the potatoes out onto the baking sheet, drizzle them with the olive oil, and sprinkle with the chopped rosemary and salt and pepper to taste. Mix together with your hands or a large spoon. Spread into an even layer.

4. Bake the potatoes, turning halfway through, until crispy and golden brown, 40 to 45 minutes. Serve garnished with a couple of sprigs of fresh rosemary and thyme.

CREAMY DILL MUSHROOMS

Serves 6 to 8

Dill mushrooms are a staple at our holiday table. Granny is *obsessed* with mushrooms. In fact, we have bought her mushroom books, mushroom ornaments, dried mushrooms for her stocking stuffers—it's a "thing" in our family. The traditional version of this dish is smothered in whipping cream, but with Cashew Cream it's just as good, we promise! If you want to stick with whipping cream, use the same amount as indicated for the Cashew Cream. These mushrooms are dynamite served with our Potato Garlic Cauliflower Mash (page 209).

1. Heat the olive oil and vegan butter in a large frying pan (preferably one with high sides) over medium heat. Add the garlic and cook, stirring, for 30 seconds. Add the white wine and cook until it's reduced by a third, 2 to 3 minutes.

2. Add the mushrooms and cook until soft, 8 to 10 minutes, stirring occasionally.

3. Add the dill and salt and pepper to taste. Stir in the Cashew Cream and serve.

GLUTEN-FREE: Use dry white wine or gluten-free vegetable stock.

2 tablespoons (30 mL) extra-virgin olive oil

2 tablespoons (30 mL) vegan butter

3 cloves garlic, crushed

½ cup (125 mL) dry white wine (we use pinot gris) or vegetable stock

2 pounds (900 g) sliced white and/or brown mushrooms (about 10 cups/2.5 L)

¼ cup (60 mL) chopped fresh dill

Salt and pepper

1 cup (250 mL) Cashew Cream (page 313)

GARLICKY GREENS

Serves 4

This is one of the easiest side dishes you will ever make. It's also the best way to get your crew to eat a heap of greens in just a few bites. These always disappear when they're put on the table! Yes, there are *a lot* of greens in this recipe, but it's amazing how much they cook down. We usually use spinach, but you can use whatever greens your heart desires—kale, Swiss chard, collard greens, beet greens, you name it. Make sure you cook these just before serving; they only take a couple of minutes to prepare and are best served hot. Serve with Potato Garlic Cauliflower Mash (page 209) for a match made in heaven!

3 tablespoons (45 mL) extra-virgin olive oil

2 large cloves garlic, crushed

12 cups (about 14 ounces/400 g) lightly packed baby spinach and/or other greens, tough stems removed, roughly chopped if large

Salt and pepper

1. Heat the olive oil in a large pot over medium heat. Add the garlic and cook, stirring, for 30 seconds, then add the greens. Gently toss with tongs or a wooden spoon and cook until the greens are slightly wilted, 2 to 3 minutes.

2. Season with salt and pepper and serve immediately.

GRILLED MEXICAN STREET CORN

Serves 5

Nothing defines summer more than fresh corn on the cob. Grilling the corn really intensifies the flavour and gives it such wow factor! You can easily change out the herbs to create your own variations. Traditional street corn has ½ cup (125 mL) of cotija (Mexican) cheese mixed in and more sprinkled on at the end, which you could easily add (or a vegan substitute) if you wish. Serve this at your next barbecue as an impressive side dish, or break the corn into 3-inch (8 cm) pieces to serve as an appetizer alongside Nacho Average Queso (page 117) and Coconut Cauliflower Tacos with Pineapple Salsa (page 113).

Soaking the corn is imperative; the husks will catch on fire if you do not soak them.

1. Gently peel the corn husks back to within 2 inches (5 cm) of the base. Remove the silk, then smooth the husks back into place, completely covering the kernels. Fill a sink with ice water and soak the corn for 30 minutes.

2. Meanwhile, in a small food processor, combine the butter, cilantro, garlic, jalapeño, lime zest, and salt; pulse until smooth. Alternatively, mash together the ingredients with a spoon in a small bowl.

3. Preheat a grill for direct cooking over medium heat.

4. Drain the corn and shake off any excess water. Peel back the husks and dry the corn with a kitchen towel. Using your hands, rub half of the butter mixture directly onto the corn cobs to lightly but evenly coat them. Smooth the husks back into place.

5. Arrange the corn directly on the grill, close the lid, and grill for 20 to 25 minutes, or until the corn is tender, turning every 5 minutes. Meanwhile, melt the remaining butter mixture.

6. Remove the corn from the grill with tongs. At this point you can either serve them as is or peel the husks back and grill the exposed cobs directly on the grill until they are slightly charred, around 5 minutes. (We recommend spraying the husks with water before grilling the exposed corn so they don't catch on fire.)

7. Carefully open the husks (if not already opened) and brush on the remaining melted butter mixture. Serve immediately.

VEGAN: Use vegan butter.

5 corn cobs, husks on (see Tip)

⅓ cup (75 mL) butter or vegan butter, at room temperature

⅓ cup (75 mL) lightly packed roughly chopped cilantro

1 clove garlic, crushed

2 teaspoons (10 mL) finely chopped jalapeño pepper

½ teaspoon (2 mL) grated fresh lime zest

½ teaspoon (2 mL) salt

1 lime, cut into wedges, for serving

TIP: If you do not want to deal with unfolding and replacing the husks and want a foolproof hack for this corn, simply boil the husked corn until tender, about 15 minutes. Lightly coat with the herb butter mixture, grill on all sides for about 15 minutes, then brush with more herb butter.

MAPLE THYME ROASTED PARSNIPS AND CARROTS

Serves 4 to 6

Roasted veggies are such an easy side dish to make, and this combination is one of our favourites. Maple syrup is a nod to our Canadian heritage and adds an earthy sweetness that caramelizes to utter perfection with the roasted vegetables. We just mix everything together on the baking sheet with our hands for easy prep because who needs extra dishes when entertaining? Serve with Mushroom Wellington (page 177) for a cozy fall meal.

1. Preheat the oven to 425°F (220°C). Line a baking sheet with parchment paper.

2. Wash and peel the parsnips and carrots. Cut them in half lengthwise and place them on the prepared baking sheet. Drizzle with the olive oil and maple syrup, then sprinkle with chopped thyme and salt and pepper to taste. Toss with your hands to combine everything, ensuring the vegetables are well coated. Spread the vegetables evenly on the baking sheet.

3. Roast, turning halfway through with a metal spatula, until golden brown and slightly caramelized, about 35 minutes.

4. Transfer the veggies to a platter, garnish with the thyme sprigs and serve immediately.

4 parsnips (about 1 pound/450 g)

6 to 7 carrots (about 1 pound/450 g)

2 tablespoons (30 mL) olive oil

2 tablespoons (30 mL) pure maple syrup

1 tablespoon (15 mL) chopped fresh thyme leaves

Salt and pepper

3 or 4 sprigs fresh thyme, for garnish

SOUTHERN PECAN SWEET POTATOES

Serves 10 to 12

Some form of sweet potatoes are a given on the Thanksgiving table, but many dishes are over-the-top sweet. We wanted to serve something that wasn't smothered in marshmallows, but still had the same nostalgic appeal! We love the different textures and familiar flavours in this dish: the sweet potatoes are creamy with a hint of warm spice, and the pecan topping adds just the right amount of sweetness and some crunch. You can make the potato mixture up to 1 day ahead, then just top it with the pecan topping (which can also be prepared in advance) and bake when you are ready.

1. Preheat the oven to 375°F (190°C).

2. MAKE THE SWEET POTATO MIXTURE Place the sweet potatoes in a large pot of water to cover and bring to a boil over medium-high heat. Cook until fork-tender, about 20 minutes. Drain in a colander and return them to the pot.

3. Mash the potatoes with a potato masher. Add the butter, brown sugar, salt to taste, cinnamon, and nutmeg. Mash again to combine. Scoop the potato mixture into a 13- × 9-inch (3 L) baking dish and smooth the top.

4. MAKE THE PECAN TOPPING Stir together the pecans, brown sugar, butter, cinnamon, and salt in a small bowl. Scatter the pecan mixture evenly over the sweet potato mixture.

5. Bake until bubbling at the edges and golden brown on top, 30 to 40 minutes. Serve hot.

VEGAN: Use vegan butter.

Sweet Potato Mixture

6 pounds (2.7 kg) sweet potatoes, peeled and cut into 1-inch (2.5 cm) cubes (4 to 5 medium potatoes)

½ cup (125 mL) butter or vegan butter

1 tablespoon (15 mL) firmly packed brown sugar

½ to 1 teaspoon (2 to 5 mL) salt

½ teaspoon (2 mL) cinnamon

¼ teaspoon (1 mL) nutmeg

Pecan Topping

1 cup (250 mL) roughly chopped raw pecans

2 tablespoons (30 mL) firmly packed brown sugar

2 tablespoons (30 mL) butter or vegan butter, melted

½ teaspoon (2 mL) cinnamon

2 pinches of salt

ROASTED ROOT VEGGIES

Serves 6 to 8

Root veggies are one of the easiest side dishes to make and can be pre-pared in a matter of minutes. The natural sugars come out of the vege-tables when they are roasted, intensifying their flavour. It's a great way to get kids to eat their veggies! You can use a variety of root veggies for this dish depending on what you find at the market. Cut them up in advance and store in a resealable bag in the fridge for a day or two. We recommend doubling the recipe so you can make a batch of Roasted Root Veggie Soup (page 143) the next day!

1. Preheat the oven to 400°F (200°C). Line a baking sheet with parchment paper.

2. Cut the root vegetables into uniform sizes, about 2-inch (5 cm) cubes. Place the vegetables on the baking sheet. Pour the olive oil over the vege-tables, sprinkle with the thyme, rosemary, and salt and pepper to taste, and massage together with your hands. Spread the vegetables evenly on the baking sheet (do not crowd them).

3. Roast until golden brown and fork-tender, about 1 hour, turning them once or twice with a metal spatula. Serve hot.

3 pounds (1.4 kg) peeled mixed root vegetables (carrots, parsnips, potatoes, sweet potatoes, rutabaga, squash)

¼ cup (60 mL) extra-virgin olive oil

1 tablespoon (15 mL) chopped fresh thyme

1 teaspoon (5 mL) chopped fresh rosemary

Salt and pepper

SUMMER HERBED GRILLED VEGETABLES

Serves 4 to 6

We prep these veggies in advance to allow the herbs and garlic to penetrate the vegetables, and that's one less thing to do before guests arrive! This is a simple but showy side dish that looks beautiful served on a platter and always impresses. Make extra to turn into Grilled Veggie Orzo Salad (page 132) the next day.

1. In a large bowl or large resealable plastic bag, combine the vegetables, garlic, basil, lemon juice, olive oil, and salt. Stir or shake the bag until all the vegetables are coated. Refrigerate for at least 1 hour or overnight.

2. Preheat a grill for direct cooking over medium heat.

3. Reserving the extra marinade in a large bowl, grill the veggies on both sides until fork-tender, 3 to 5 minutes per side. Transfer the grilled vegetables to the bowl and toss with the marinade before serving.

6 cups (1.5 L) mixed vegetables cut into ½-inch (1 cm) thick slices or large pieces (we use zucchini, sweet onion, fennel, and a mix of red, yellow, and orange sweet peppers)

3 large cloves garlic, crushed

1 cup (250 mL) loosely packed fresh basil, chopped

¼ cup (60 mL) fresh lemon juice

¼ cup (60 mL) extra-virgin olive oil

1 teaspoon (5 mL) salt

JILLY'S ALMOST FAMOUS STUFFING

Serves 8

Turkey stuffing, meet your match. Tori's mom, Patsy, was (and still is) the stuffing queen and was responsible for teaching Jilly how to master this dish. Her version had breakfast sausage in it and no white wine or apple. This un-stuffed stuffing will win over everyone at the holiday table! It's moist, packed with all of those familiar stuffing flavours (addictive, actually), and super simple to put together. Double this recipe and use the same pan if you are feeding a crowd. Serve along-side Southern Pecan Sweet Potatoes (page 221), Mushroom Wellington (page 177), Vegan Perogies (page 243), and all the other holiday fixings.

1. Preheat the oven to 350°F (180°C). Grease a 10-inch (25 cm) round or 10½- × 7½-inch (2.3 L) rectangular baking dish.

2. Heat the vegan butter and olive oil in a large frying pan over medium heat. Add the celery and onions and cook until soft and fragrant, 3 to 4 minutes, stirring occasionally.

3. Add the garlic, mushrooms, sage, and thyme and cook, stirring occasionally, until the mushrooms are soft, 8 to 10 minutes.

4. Stir in the apple, white wine, poultry seasoning, salt and pepper. Cook for 3 to 5 minutes, until the apple slightly softens. Add 1 cup (250 mL) of the vegetable stock, stir, and cook for another 3 minutes.

5. Place the bread cubes in a large bowl. Pour the mushroom mixture over the bread and lightly toss with a rubber spatula to combine. Drizzle with additional stock if you prefer a moister stuffing, and season with additional poultry seasoning, salt, and pepper, if desired.

6. Spread the stuffing evenly in the prepared baking dish and bake until heated through, about 30 minutes. Serve immediately.

½ cup (125 mL) vegan butter

¼ cup (60 mL) extra-virgin olive oil

2 cups (500 mL) finely chopped celery (3 to 4 stalks)

1½ cups (375 mL) finely chopped yellow onions (1 medium onion)

4 cloves garlic, crushed

1 pound (450 g) finely chopped white and/or brown mushrooms (about 4 cups/1 L)

2 tablespoons (30 mL) chopped fresh sage

2 teaspoons (10 mL) fresh thyme leaves

1 Granny Smith apple, unpeeled and finely diced

¼ cup (60 mL) white wine (we use chardonnay)

4 teaspoons (20 mL) poultry seasoning

½ teaspoon (2 mL) salt

½ teaspoon (2 mL) pepper

1 to 1½ cups (250 to 375 mL) vegetable stock

1 loaf day-old white bread, roughly cut into 1-inch (2.5 cm) cubes

MUSHROOM GRAVY

Serves 8 to 10

This gravy takes a bit of work but is well worth the effort. Rich and earthy, thanks to the mushrooms, it is super decadent poured over Potato Garlic Cauliflower Mash (page 209) or with Jilly's Almost Famous Stuffing (page 227). It can be made ahead and reheated, a blessing in that last-minute scramble to get everything on the table!

1. Heat the olive oil in a large frying pan over medium heat. Add the garlic and mushrooms and cook until the mushrooms start to soften, about 8 minutes, stirring occasionally. Stir in the sage, parsley, and thyme and continue to cook for 5 minutes, stirring occasionally. Transfer the mixture to a medium bowl and set aside.

2. In the same pan, melt the vegan butter over medium heat. Add the onions and cook until soft and turning a light golden brown, stirring occasionally, 6 to 8 minutes.

3. Sprinkle the flour over the onions and stir constantly with a wooden spoon to cook the flour, 5 to 7 minutes: you are looking for a light brown colour with a slightly nutty aroma.

4. While whisking, slowly add 1½ cups (375 mL) of the vegetable stock and the Cashew Cream to the flour mixture, and whisk to combine. Add the mushroom mixture, stir well, and season with salt and pepper.

5. Scrape the mixture into a large bowl. Carefully blend until smooth using an immersion blender. Alternatively, let cool slightly and then purée in a blender. Add additional stock if needed to thin the gravy and serve.

GLUTEN-FREE: Use gluten-free vegetable stock and omit the flour; skip step 3. Instead, mix 4 teaspoons (20 mL) of cornstarch into 3 tablespoons (45 mL) of water and add the cornstarch mixture at the end of step 4, stirring constantly and bringing the gravy to a simmer until it thickens, 1 to 2 minutes.

2 tablespoons (30 mL) extra-virgin olive oil

2 cloves garlic, crushed

12 ounces (340 g) sliced white and/or brown mushrooms (about 4 cups/1 L)

1 tablespoon (15 mL) finely chopped fresh sage

1 tablespoon (15 mL) finely chopped fresh flat-leaf parsley

1 teaspoon (5 mL) fresh thyme leaves

2 tablespoons (30 mL) vegan butter

¾ cup (175 mL) finely chopped yellow onion (1 small onion)

3 tablespoons (45 mL) all-purpose flour

1½ to 2 cups (375 to 500 mL) vegetable stock

½ cup (125 mL) Cashew Cream (page 313)

Salt and pepper

SKILLET CORNBREAD

Serves 6 to 8

Baking cornbread in a skillet gives it a crispy exterior and an amazing rustic presentation that we love! This cornbread is ever so slightly sweet, with a kick of heat from the chili peppers, and is nice and moist thanks to the creamed corn. Cornbread is a family favourite, and with Jill's dad's chili in the cookbook, how could we not have a cornbread recipe? Jill recalls taking her mom to one of her favourite Chicago restaurants, Hub 51, and her mom obsessing over their cornbread. When we decided that cornbread had to be in the book, Jill knew the person to ask for the recipe (we modified it slightly, but it's pretty close!). Serve alongside Vegetarian Chili (page 184) for a hearty meal.

1. Preheat the oven to 400°F (200°C). Brush a medium cast-iron frying pan with oil.

2. In a large bowl, beat together the butter and sugar using an electric mixer on medium-high speed until light and fluffy. Add the eggs one at a time, mixing until incorporated.

3. In a medium bowl, sift together the flour, baking powder, and salt. Add the flour mixture, cornmeal, creamed corn, and milk to the butter mixture and beat with the electric mixer on medium speed just until completely mixed. Fold in the canned corn and chili peppers (if using).

4. Scrape the batter into the prepared frying pan and bake until the edges are golden brown and a toothpick inserted into the centre comes out clean, about 30 minutes.

5. Cut the cornbread into wedges and serve warm.

DAIRY-FREE: Use vegan butter and unsweetened almond milk or unsweetened soy milk.

½ cup (125 mL) butter or vegan butter, at room temperature

½ cup (125 mL) sugar

2 eggs, at room temperature

1 cups (250 mL) all-purpose flour

1 tablespoon (15 mL) baking powder

½ teaspoon (2 mL) salt

1½ cups (375 mL) yellow cornmeal

¾ cup (175 mL) canned creamed corn

½ cup (125 mL) 2% milk or unsweetened dairy-free milk

1 cup (250 mL) drained canned corn kernels or frozen corn kernels

¼ cup (60 mL) canned diced chili peppers or pickled jalapeño peppers (optional)

MOLASSES OATMEAL BREAD

Makes 2 loaves

There's something so cathartic about making your own bread: we swear it's better than therapy! This bread is so moist, delicious, and incredibly old-fashioned. We highly recommend serving it alongside Granny's Overhauled Baked Beans (page 183) warm out of the oven. You can freeze any extras (we recommend pre-slicing it) for an epic slice of toast on those busy mornings.

1. Grease two 8- × 4-inch (1.5 L) loaf pans with olive oil or vegetable oil.

2. In a large bowl, combine the oats, molasses, honey, butter, and salt. Add the boiling water and stir well. Let stand for about 1 hour at room temperature (it can be left uncovered).

3. Place the warm water in a small bowl, sprinkle the yeast over it, and stir to dissolve. Let stand until foamy, 5 to 10 minutes.

4. Add the whole wheat flour along with the yeast mixture to the cooled oat mixture and stir until combined. Add 1 cup (250 mL) of the all-purpose flour, stir, and continue adding more flour, 1 cup (250 mL) at a time, kneading the flour into the dough with the palms of your hands until the dough sticks together. Turn the dough out onto a well-floured work surface and continue to knead, adding small amounts of all-purpose flour while you knead, until the dough is smooth and elastic, about 10 minutes.

5. Place the dough in a large, oiled bowl, cover with a kitchen towel, and let the dough rise in a warm, draft-free area until doubled in size, about 1 hour.

6. Tip the dough out onto a lightly floured work surface and gently deflate it using your hands. Cut the dough in half. Using a lightly floured rolling pin, gently roll out 1 portion of dough into a rectangle. Starting at the long end, roll the dough up completely, gently pressing the seam into the roll using the palms of your hands. Tuck the ends in just enough so that the loaf fits into the pan, press gently on the new seams with the palms of your hands, and place the loaf seam-side down in a prepared pan. Repeat with the remaining portion of dough. Cover each pan with a kitchen towel, and let rise in a warm, draft-free area until doubled in size, about 1 hour.

1 cup (250 mL) old-fashioned rolled oats

⅓ cup (75 mL) fancy molasses

2 tablespoons (30 mL) pure liquid honey or maple syrup

1 tablespoon (15 mL) butter or vegan butter

2 teaspoons (10 mL) salt

2 cups (500 mL) boiling water

½ cup (125 mL) lukewarm water (100 to 110°F/38 to 43°C)

1 tablespoon (15 mL) active dry yeast (one 8 g package)

2½ cups (575 mL) whole wheat flour

2 to 3 cups (500 to 750 mL) all-purpose flour

Continued . . .

Molasses Oatmeal Bread continued

7. While the dough rises, preheat the oven to 375°F (190°C).

8. Bake the loaves until they are golden brown and sound hollow when tapped, 30 to 40 minutes. Remove the loaves from the pans and let cool completely on racks before serving. Store in a plastic bag at room temperature for up to 3 days or in the freezer for up to 2 weeks.

VEGAN: Use vegan butter and use maple syrup instead of honey.

BISCUITS THREE WAYS

Makes 8 biscuits

Served alongside a bowl of steaming soup, these biscuits of Tori's have been a family staple for years. Let this recipe be your blank canvas once you feel you have mastered the plain biscuits. The possibilities are endless: you can honestly fold in so many different ingredients (herbs like dill, or sweet ingredients like dried apricots or fresh sliced plums with 1 tablespoon (15 mL) of sugar added to the dry ingredients for the sweet variations). We have even included a vegan version! The trick to a good biscuit is to not overhandle the dough and to make sure your butter is as cold as possible. These biscuits are best served hot out of the oven. Try them with our Roasted Root Veggie Soup (page 143). See the following page for our variations.

1. Preheat the oven to 450°F (230°C). Line a baking sheet with parchment paper.

2. In a small liquid measuring cup, whisk the egg. Add the milk to the ¾-cup (175 mL) mark and whisk to combine.

3. In a large bowl, combine the flour, baking powder, and salt; whisk to combine. Add the butter and, using your fingers or a pastry blender, break up the butter until the pieces are the size of peas.

4. Add the milk mixture to the flour mixture and gently mix together with a rubber spatula until just combined (don't overmix!). The dough should just stick together but look rough. If your dough is too dry, add 1 to 2 additional tablespoons (15 to 30 mL) of milk. Scrape the dough out onto a lightly floured work surface. Pat and gently shape the dough until it sticks together in a disc about 1½ inches (4 cm) thick.

5. Using a sharp knife, cut into 8 triangles. Transfer the biscuits to the prepared baking sheet. Bake until golden brown, 15 to 20 minutes. Serve immediately.

1 egg, at room temperature

½ to ¾ cup (125 to 175 mL) 2% milk or unsweetened almond milk

2 cups (500 mL) all-purpose flour

4 teaspoons (20 mL) baking powder

¼ teaspoon (1 mL) salt

5 tablespoons (75 mL) cold butter or vegan butter, cubed

Continued . . .

Biscuits Three Ways continued

CHEDDAR CHIVE BISCUITS

1. Stir 1 cup (250 mL) of the cheese and the chives into the flour mixture in step 3. Sprinkle the remaining ⅓ cup (75 mL) cheese on top of the biscuits after the biscuits are cut and just before baking.

1⅓ cups (325 mL) shredded aged cheddar cheese or vegan cheddar cheese, divided

¼ cup (60 mL) thinly sliced fresh chives

CURRANT OR RAISIN BISCUITS

1. Add the sugar to the flour mixture in step 3. Fold in the currants or raisins after working in the butter in step 3.

¼ cup (60 mL) sugar

¾ cup (175 mL) dried currants or raisins

VEGAN: Omit the egg; use the full ¾ cup (175 mL) unsweetened almond milk instead of the 2% milk. Use vegan butter. Use vegan cheese for the Cheddar Chive Biscuits.

a

b

c

d

PERFECT WHITE BUNS

Makes 24 buns

Each of our family members have a dish that we are in charge of bringing to our holiday dinners. Tori always make the buns. She tweaked this recipe passed down from our sweet auntie Jackie, and it makes *the* most soft, fluffy, delicious buns. Homemade bread will impress anyone, and it is not as difficult as you might think. Making bread is really a lot about feel, so it's important to make sure that you only add enough flour to keep the dough from being sticky and to stop once you reach that point. Adding too much flour will yield a dry bread. We typically eat whole grain bread, so these white buns are a real indulgence for those special holidays, but Tori's buns really are the best!

3 tablespoons (45 mL) butter or vegan butter

2 tablespoons (30 mL) pure liquid honey

2 teaspoons (10 mL) salt

1½ cups (375 mL) boiling water

1 tablespoon (15 mL) sugar

1½ cups (375 mL) warm water

2 tablespoons (30 mL) fast-rising dry yeast (two 8 g packages)

5 to 6 cups (1.25 to 1.5 L) all-purpose flour, divided

1. In a large bowl, combine the butter, honey, and salt. Add the boiling water, stir, and let sit, uncovered, to cool until lukewarm.

2. In a liquid measuring cup, stir the sugar into the warm water until dissolved. Sprinkle the yeast evenly on top and let sit for 5 minutes, until it bubbles.

3. Once the water and butter mixture has cooled, add 1 cup (250 mL) of the flour. Stir well with a wooden spoon. Add the yeast mixture and stir to combine. Add 4 cups (1 L) flour and stir until you cannot stir with a spoon (it will get too difficult).

4. Scrape the dough out onto a well-floured surface and knead for about 10 minutes, until smooth and elastic. Add small amounts of flour, up to 1 cup (250 mL), as you knead the dough to keep it from sticking to your hands and the work surface. The dough should feel soft, not stiff.

5. Place the dough in a large well-oiled bowl, cover with a kitchen towel, and let the dough rise in a warm, draft-free area until doubled in size, 45 to 60 minutes. Gently deflate the dough. Cover and let rise for another 30 minutes.

Continued . . .

6. While the dough rises, preheat the oven to 350°F (180°C). Grease a baking sheet or cake pans with extra-virgin olive oil, butter or vegan butter.

7. Gently deflate the dough. Tip the dough out onto a lightly floured surface and divide it into 24 equal pieces (about ⅔ cup/150 mL each). Shape the dough pieces into balls, tucking the edges under to make the tops smooth. Evenly space the buns about ½ inch (1 cm) apart on the baking sheet. (Or you can nestle the buns in cake pans; 8 buns per pan display nicely.) Cover with a kitchen towel and let rise until doubled, about 45 minutes.

8. Bake until golden brown, 15 to 20 minutes. Transfer the buns to a rack and let cool completely. If you used cake pans, flip the pans upside-down to remove the buns and let cool on a rack.

VEGAN: Use vegan butter and use sugar instead of honey.

VEGAN PEROGIES

Makes about 50 perogies

Perogies are a *must* at any of our big family celebrations. We always thought there was some sort of wizardry that went into making them, but they are actually easy—just a bit time-consuming. This is such a fun project to take on with a group over coffee or a glass of wine—they are pure therapy to make and even more so to eat! We always serve our perogies with sour cream, but you can use Vegan Sour Cream (page 315). Pan-frying the boiled perogies takes them to another level. Feel free to switch it up and fill them with sauerkraut instead of potato filling.

1. MAKE THE DOUGH Combine the water and vegetable oil in a large bowl and whisk together.

2. Add 4 cups (1 L) of the flour along with the salt and mix together with a wooden spoon. Turn the dough out onto a well-floured work surface and knead, gradually adding up to 1 cup (250 mL) more flour, to make a firm dough that is not sticky.

3. Place the ball of dough in a medium, lightly greased bowl (use olive oil or vegan butter), cover with a damp kitchen towel, and let rest for 30 minutes.

4. MEANWHILE, MAKE THE FILLING In a small frying pan, heat 2 tablespoons (30 mL) of the vegan butter over medium-low heat. Add the onions and cook, stirring occasionally, until golden brown and soft, about 20 minutes. Remove from the heat and set aside.

5. Meanwhile, bring 2 large pots of water to a boil. In one pot, boil the potatoes until very soft, about 15 minutes. Drain the potatoes in a colander and return them to the pot. Add the remaining 2 tablespoons (30 mL) vegan butter and salt and mash the potatoes until they are smooth. Stir in the cooked onions, nutritional yeast, and pepper to taste. Add more salt if needed.

Dough

½ cup (125 mL) water

¼ cup (60 mL) vegetable oil

4 to 5 cups (1 to 1.25 L) all-purpose flour

1 teaspoon (5 mL) salt

Filling

4 tablespoons (60 mL) vegan butter, divided

2 cups (500 mL) finely chopped yellow onion (1 large onion)

3 pounds (1.4 kg) red potatoes, peeled and cubed

1 teaspoon (5 mL) salt, more if needed

¼ cup (60 mL) nutritional yeast

Pepper

Topping

2 tablespoons (30 mL) vegan butter

1 cup (250 mL) finely chopped yellow onion (1 medium)

Vegan Sour Cream (page 315), for serving

Continued . . .

a

b

c

d

6. Once the dough has rested, divide it in half. On a lightly floured surface and using a lightly floured rolling pin, roll out one piece of dough until it is about ⅛ inch (3 mm) thick. Cut out circles using a 2- to 2½-inch (5 to 6 cm) cookie cutter, or simply cut the dough into circles or squares using a sharp knife. (There's less waste if you use a knife. You *can* reroll the dough scraps, but it gets tough.)

7. Place a piece of the cut-out dough in your hand and put 1 teaspoon (5 mL) of the filling in the centre of the dough. Fold the dough over the filling to create a pocket and carefully pinch the edges of the dough together with your fingers to seal. Repeat with the remaining dough, setting the finished perogies on a kitchen towel or a baking sheet lined with parchment paper. (You can freeze the perogies on a cookie sheet and then store them in a resealable plastic bag in the freezer for up to 2 months. You can cook them straight from the freezer.)

8. Working in batches so you don't overcrowd the perogies, gently drop the perogies into the second pot of boiling water and boil for 5 to 7 minutes; the perogies will float to the surface when cooked. Remove them with a slotted spoon, place in a large, oiled bowl, and repeat until all the perogies are cooked.

9. WHILE THE PEROGIES ARE COOKING, PREPARE THE ONIONS FOR TOPPING Melt the vegan butter in a small frying pan over medium-low heat. Add the onions and cook, stirring occasionally, until soft and golden brown, about 20 minutes.

10. Transfer the cooked perogies to a serving bowl and toss them with the onion mixture, or lightly fry them in a nonstick pan with a bit of olive oil or vegan butter. Serve hot with sour cream or Vegan Sour Cream.

UKRAINIAN SAVOURY CREPES

Serves 6 to 8

Nalysnyky (pronounced nah-less-knee-kee) are traditional Ukrainian crepes with a number of different fillings. We make them with a delicious cottage cheese dill filling and usually serve them at Easter. Tori's mom has perfected them over the years working off of an old recipe that came from our great-granny Reesik.

1. MAKE THE CREPE BATTER In a blender, combine the flour, eggs, milk, butter, sugar, and salt. Blend until smooth. Let sit for at least 1 hour or up to overnight.

2. MEANWHILE, MAKE THE COTTAGE CHEESE FILLING Heat the butter and vegetable oil in a small frying pan over medium-low heat. Add the green onions and cook until fragrant, 1 to 2 minutes, stirring occasionally. Set aside to cool.

3. Place the dry cottage cheese in a medium bowl and mash it with a fork. Add the cooked green onions, egg yolks, dill, salt, and pepper and mix well.

4. MAKE THE CREPES Lightly brush an 8-inch (20 cm) crepe pan or nonstick frying pan with vegetable oil and heat over medium heat. Pour in about ¼ cup (60 mL) of the crepe batter, quickly swirl the pan so that the batter spreads evenly over the bottom, and cook until the bottom is light brown, 2 to 3 minutes. Flip and cook for 30 to 60 seconds, then transfer to a plate. Repeat with the remaining crepes, brushing the pan with oil between each crepe, and stacking the cooked crepes on the plate. Let the crepes cool to room temperature.

5. Preheat the oven to 350°F (180°C). Lightly grease a 13- × 9-inch (3 L) baking dish with vegetable oil.

6. Spread a heaping tablespoon of the cottage cheese filling evenly in the centre of a crepe, leaving a 1-inch (2.5 cm) border around the edges. Tightly roll up the crepe halfway, then tuck in 1 inch (2.5 cm) of the sides and continue rolling. Place the crepe in the prepared pan seam side down. Repeat with the remaining crepes and filling, tucking the finished crepes tightly next to each other.

7. Pour the cream evenly over the crepes. Bake until the cream is bubbling and the tops of the crepes just start to turn a light golden brown, about 20 minutes. Serve hot with fresh dill and sour cream.

Crepes

2 cups (500 mL) all-purpose flour

3 eggs

2½ cups (575 mL) 2% milk or unsweetened almond milk

¼ cup (60 mL) butter or vegan butter, melted

2 teaspoons (10 mL) sugar

½ teaspoon (2 mL) salt

Vegetable oil or avocado oil, for cooking

Cottage Cheese Filling

1 tablespoon (15 mL) butter or vegan butter

1 teaspoon (5 mL) vegetable oil or avocado oil

4 green onions, thinly sliced

1 tub (21 ounces/600 g) dry cottage cheese

2 egg yolks, beaten

¼ cup (60 mL) finely chopped fresh dill, more for serving

½ teaspoon (2 mL) salt

¼ teaspoon (1 mL) pepper

1 cup (250 mL) table (18%) cream

Sour cream or Vegan Sour Cream (page page 315), for serving

NUT-FREE: Use 2% milk.

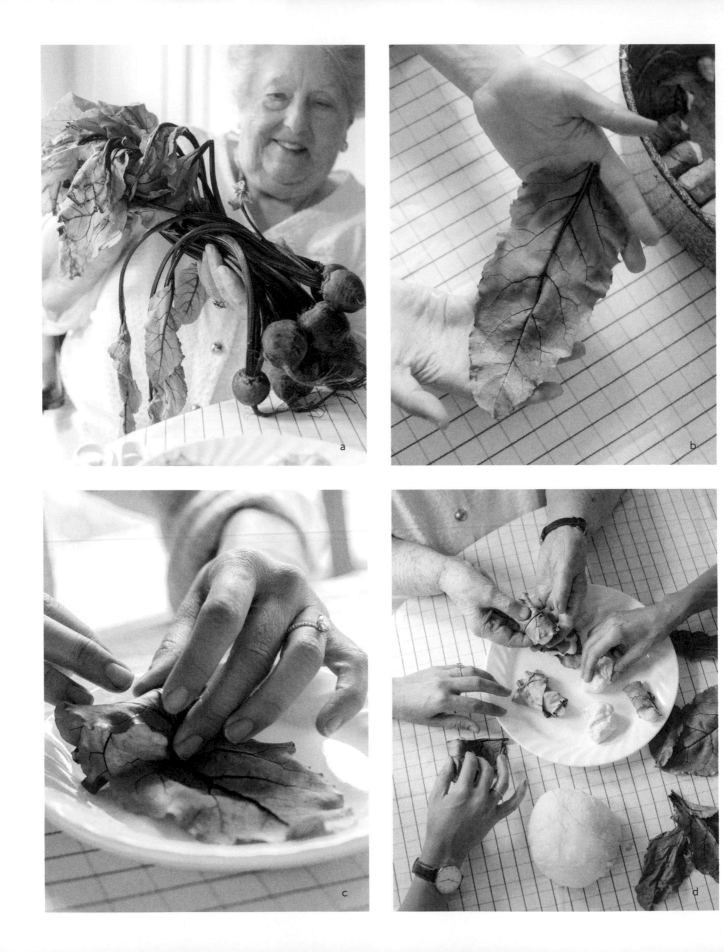

GRANNY'S BEET ROLLS

Serves 12 to 14

Our granny Marg is nicknamed the Beet Roll Queen for good reason: she *loves* to make beet rolls. Before any big holiday, you can find her at her kitchen table with a giant batch of fresh bread dough and a mountain of beet leaves just rolling away to the sound of Johnny Cash in the background. Beet rolls are a traditional Ukrainian dish and they are simply addictive. Of course, Granny's version is rather rich (putting it mildly). We are including both versions here, the real deal along with a vegan version.

   You'll need a large roasting pan with a lid for this dish and a good amount of time, as they take a while to make. We don't do this traditionally, but some people put chopped fresh dill in the whipping cream before pouring it on or add it to the sour cream before serving. Either would taste amazing!

1. Generously grease a large roasting pan with butter or olive oil.

2. Pull off a golf-ball size piece of dough. Place it on a beet leaf and roll up the leaf (the dough may slightly stick out the ends—that's okay). Place the beet roll seam side down in the roasting pan. Repeat with the remaining dough and beet leaves, fitting the rolls snugly in the pan (they should be touching), until the bottom of the pan is covered in a layer of beet rolls. You should have used up half of the beet leaves and dough at this stage. Sprinkle the rolls with ½ teaspoon (2 mL) of the salt.

3. Repeat with the remaining dough and beet leaves to make a second layer, again fitting them in snugly so that they touch each other. Sprinkle the remaining ½ teaspoon (2 mL) salt over the rolls. Cover with the lid and let it rise until they have doubled in size, 2 to 3 hours.

4. Preheat the oven to 350°F (180°C).

I batch Perfect White Buns dough (page 239)

80 to 90 clean, dry wilted medium beet leaves (see Tip)

I teaspoon (5 mL) salt, divided

3 cups (750 mL) whipping (35%) cream, at room temperature

Sour cream, for serving (optional)

TIP: After washing the beet leaves, lay them (without overlapping) on kitchen towels, cover them with another kitchen towel, and leave them on the counter for 3 to 4 hours to dry and wilt. This makes them easier to roll.

Continued . . .

Granny's Beet Rolls continued

5. Slowly pour the whipping cream evenly over the beet rolls. Bake the beet rolls, uncovered, until they are golden brown, about 1 hour. Serve with sour cream (if using).

VEGAN: Use the vegan version of the bun dough. Omit the whipping cream. Once baked, pour 1 cup (250 mL) melted vegan butter mixed with 2 cups (500 mL) Cashew Cream (page 313) evenly over the beet rolls. Bake, uncovered, for an additional 5 minutes. Alternatively, you can pan-fry the cooked beet rolls (once slightly cooled) in the same vegan butter and Cashew Cream mixture (instead of pouring it on top), tossing and cooking in a large pan in two batches over medium heat until they are crisp and golden (and so delicious!). Serve with our Vegan Sour Cream (page 315).

DESSERTS

VEGETARIAN / DAIRY-FREE OPTION / NUT-FREE OPTION

IRISH APPLE CAKE

Makes one 8-inch (20 cm) round cake; serves 10 to 12

While we love summer, there is something incredibly cozy about fall.
The crisp air, the leaves turning, cable-knit sweaters, and of course,
boatloads of fresh apples looking for a home. This easy cake uses two
types of apples for added texture and is moist, filled with fall spices,
and finished with a crunchy streusel. Serve with ice cream or dairy-free
ice cream, or take it to the next level with a drizzle of Vegan Caramel
Sauce (page 256). Jillian's beau Justin's mom, Melissa, is Irish, and we
loved that we could create a recipe that's a nod to her heritage!

1. Preheat the oven to 350°F (180°C). Grease and flour an 8-inch (20 cm)
round cake pan.

2. PREPARE THE STREUSEL In a medium bowl, combine the whole
wheat flour, pecans, brown sugar, cinnamon, and salt. Add the butter and
stir until combined. Set aside.

3. MAKE THE APPLE CAKE In a large bowl, combine the butter, white
cane sugar, and brown sugar. Beat using an electric mixer on medium
speed. Add the eggs, one at a time, beating well after each addition. Add
the vanilla and beat until smooth.

4. In a separate medium bowl, combine the all-purpose flour, whole wheat
flour, baking powder, baking soda, salt, cinnamon, nutmeg, and cloves.
Whisk to combine. Add to the wet ingredients and beat on medium speed
until combined.

5. Stir in the Spartan and Granny Smith apples to combine. Scrape the
batter into the prepared cake pan, smoothing the top. Spread the Streusel
evenly over the cake.

6. Bake until lightly browned and a toothpick inserted into the centre
comes out clean, about 45 minutes. Let cool in the pan on a rack for
20 minutes before removing from the pan and cooling completely. Store
covered at room temperature for up to 3 days.

DAIRY-FREE: Use vegan butter.

NUT-FREE: Skip the pecans.

Streusel

¼ cup (60 mL) whole wheat flour

⅓ cup (75 mL) chopped raw
pecans

¼ cup (60 mL) firmly packed
brown sugar

½ teaspoon (2 mL) cinnamon

Pinch of salt

2 tablespoons + 1½ teaspoons
(37 mL) butter or vegan
butter, melted

Apple Cake

½ cup (125 mL) butter or vegan
butter

½ cup (125 mL) white cane sugar

¼ cup (60 mL) firmly packed
brown sugar

2 eggs

1 teaspoon (5 mL) pure vanilla
extract

1 cup (250 mL) all-purpose flour

½ cup (125 mL) whole wheat flour

1 teaspoon (5 mL) baking powder

½ teaspoon (2 mL) baking soda

¼ teaspoon (1 mL) salt

1 teaspoon (5 mL) cinnamon

¼ teaspoon (1 mL) nutmeg

Pinch of ground cloves

1½ cups (375 mL) peeled, cored,
and shredded Spartan or
Gala apples (2 apples)

1½ cups (375 mL) peeled, cored,
and thinly sliced Granny
Smith apples (2 apples)

VEGAN CARAMEL SAUCE

Makes 1 cup (250 mL)

A typical caramel sauce takes a bit of work and involves some candy-making science. This version skips a few steps but still yields a delicious thick, rich sauce—and it's vegan! This recipe grew out of a fortuitous mistake. Tori was recipe-testing a caramel sauce at Jill's house but couldn't find any whipping cream. Jillian suggested she try coconut cream instead, and voilà, pure amazingness! And dare we say it's better than the original. It tastes fantastic on Irish Apple Cake (page 255) or Black Bean Coconut Brownies (page 280).

1. Place the flour in a small bowl and slowly whisk in the coconut cream, whisking until there are no lumps. Pour the mixture through a fine sieve to remove any remaining lumps.

2. In a small saucepan over medium heat, combine the brown sugar and vegan butter. Bring to a simmer, stirring. Slowly whisk in the coconut cream mixture, then add the vanilla and salt. Cook, stirring constantly, until it bubbles and thickens, 2 to 3 minutes.

3. Set aside to cool. Store in a resealable container in the fridge for up to 1 week.

GLUTEN-FREE: Use 1½ teaspoons (7 mL) cornstarch to replace the flour.

1 tablespoon (15 mL) all-purpose flour

⅓ cup (75 mL) coconut cream

½ cup (125 mL) firmly packed brown sugar

3 tablespoons (45 mL) vegan butter

1 teaspoon (5 mL) pure vanilla extract

¼ teaspoon (1 mL) sea salt

CITRUS OLIVE OIL BUNDT CAKE

Makes one 10-inch (25 cm) Bundt cake; serves 12 to 14

This cake . . . where do we begin? We have never tested a recipe more times to get it just right, and we think we nailed it, if we do say so ourselves. A breeze to make, super showy, moist (thank you, olive oil), and bursting with citrus flavour, it will also make your house smell like a million dollars! Make sure that the cake is completely cooled before drizzling on the glaze. Alternatively, you can skip the glaze altogether and simply dust the cake with icing sugar.

1. MAKE THE CITRUS OLIVE OIL BUNDT CAKE Preheat the oven to 350°F (180°C). Spray a 10-inch (25 cm) Bundt pan with nonstick baking spray or brush with olive oil.

2. In a large bowl, combine the flour, sugar, baking powder, baking soda, and salt. Whisk until combined.

3. In a medium bowl, combine the eggs, olive oil, honey, lemon zest, orange zest, lemon juice, orange juice, and vanilla. Whisk until smooth. Add to the flour mixture and whisk just until combined (do not overmix the batter, or the cake will not be as tender).

4. Pour the batter into the prepared Bundt pan and bake until a toothpick inserted into the centre comes out clean, 25 to 30 minutes. Let the cake sit for 10 minutes before turning it out onto a rack to cool completely.

5. MAKE THE CITRUS GLAZE In a small bowl, whisk together the icing sugar, lemon zest, lemon juice, and orange zest. Using a spoon, drizzle the glaze over the top of the cooled cake before serving. Store, covered, at room temperature for up to 3 days.

Citrus Olive Oil Bundt Cake

3 cups (750 mL) all-purpose flour

¾ cup (175 mL) sugar

2 teaspoons (10 mL) baking powder

2 teaspoons (10 mL) baking soda

½ teaspoon (2 mL) salt

3 eggs, beaten

1 cup (250 mL) extra-virgin olive oil

½ cup (125 mL) pure liquid honey

¼ cup (60 mL) packed lemon zest (from 4 to 5 lemons)

3 tablespoons (45 mL) orange zest (from 2 to 3 large oranges)

½ cup (125 mL) fresh lemon juice

¼ cup (60 mL) fresh orange juice

2 teaspoons (10 mL) pure vanilla extract

Citrus Glaze

½ cup (125 mL) icing sugar

1 teaspoon (5 mL) grated fresh lemon zest

2 tablespoons (30 mL) fresh lemon juice

1 teaspoon (5 mL) grated fresh orange zest

PEGGY'S CHOCOLATE CAKE

Makes one 8-inch (20 cm) round two-layer cake; serves 10 to 12

Tori created most of the desserts in this book—she is the baker in the family—Jillian is not really a sweets person. She rarely gets a birthday cake simply because she doesn't even like cake. That is, until *this* cake! Whenever Jillian's mom, Peggy, makes this chocolate cake, Jillian could seriously polish off the entire thing. Peggy's cake is the easiest, moistest chocolate cake around! Be sure to use Dutch-processed dark cocoa powder for the richest, darkest cake and icing.

1. MAKE THE CHOCOLATE CAKE Preheat the oven to 350°F (180°C). Grease and flour two 8-inch (20 cm) round cake pans.

2. In a large bowl, sift together the sugar, flour, cocoa powder, baking soda, and salt.

3. In a medium bowl, whisk together the eggs, water, avocado oil, mayonnaise, and vanilla. Add the wet ingredients to the dry ingredients and whisk together to combine.

4. Divide the batter evenly between the prepared pans and bake until a toothpick inserted into the centre comes out clean, 35 to 40 minutes. Let cool in the pans on a rack for 10 minutes before turning the cakes out onto the rack to cool completely.

5. MEANWHILE, MAKE THE CHOCOLATE ICING In a medium bowl and using an electric mixer on high speed, cream the butter. Add the icing sugar, cocoa powder, and almond extract and beat well. Add the almond milk, 1 tablespoon (15 mL) at a time, until the icing is a smooth, spreadable consistency.

6. Once the cakes are completely cool, level off the tops, if needed, with a sharp bread knife, holding it as straight as possible horizontally to create 2 even cake layers.

7. Place one layer on a cake pedestal or cake plate. Evenly spread ½ cup (125 mL) of the Chocolate Icing on top of the cake layer. Place the other cake layer cut side down on top of the iced layer and carefully spread the remaining icing over the cake using a knife or thin metal spatula. Store, covered, at room temperature for 2 to 3 days.

DAIRY-FREE: Use vegan butter.

Chocolate Cake

2 cups (500 mL) sugar

2 cups (500 mL) all-purpose flour

1 cup (250 mL) Dutch-processed dark cocoa powder

2 teaspoons (10 mL) baking soda

½ teaspoon (2 mL) salt

2 eggs

2 cups (500 mL) water

⅓ cup (75 mL) avocado oil or vegetable oil

2 tablespoons (30 mL) mayonnaise or vegan mayonnaise

2 teaspoons (10 mL) pure vanilla extract

Chocolate Icing

½ cup (125 mL) butter or vegan butter, at room temperature

2 cups (500 mL) icing sugar, sifted

⅓ cup (75 mL) Dutch-processed dark cocoa powder, sifted

1 teaspoon (5 mL) pure almond extract or pure vanilla extract

1 to 2 tablespoons (15 to 30 mL) unsweetened almond milk

PEACHES AND CREAM SHORTCAKES

Serves 6

These shortcakes are all about the fruit, so choose the ripest, juiciest peaches you can get your hands on in the summer. This sweet, uncomplicated, and old-fashioned dessert lets the fruit be the star. We love how quickly these come together, it's a perfect recipe to have in your back pocket for a classy summer dessert. These shortcakes are traditionally served with real whipped cream, which you could substitute for the coconut whipped topping if no one is avoiding dairy. You can substitute another soft fresh fruit such as plums, strawberries, nectarines, or raspberries if peaches aren't in season. The shortcakes are best served the day they're made, otherwise they will dry out.

1. Preheat the oven to 425°F (220°C). Line a baking sheet with parchment paper.

2. In a large bowl, sift together the flour, ¼ cup (60 mL) of the sugar, baking powder, and salt. Add the cold vegan butter and lightly mix it into the flour mixture with a pastry blender or your fingers until the pieces of butter are the size of peas.

3. Add the almond milk and toss with a fork until just combined (do not overmix the dough!).

4. Turn the dough out onto a lightly floured work surface, and pat it out to ¾-inch (2 cm) thickness. Using a 3-inch (8 cm) round cookie cutter or a small glass, cut out 6 biscuits.

5. Arrange the biscuits evenly on the prepared baking sheet. Brush the tops with almond milk and sprinkle with the remaining 2 tablespoons (30 mL) sugar. Bake until the biscuits are lightly browned, 20 to 25 minutes. Transfer to a rack to cool completely.

6. Once the biscuits are cool, cut each one in half. Place a bottom half on each plate, top with a spoonful of peaches, a dollop of coconut whipped topping, and a drizzle of honey. Serve with the top half of the biscuit and a couple of sprigs of thyme.

VEGAN: Use maple syrup instead of honey.

2 cups (500 mL) all-purpose flour

¼ cup (60 mL) + 2 tablespoons (30 mL) sugar, divided

4 teaspoons (20 mL) baking powder

½ teaspoon (2 mL) salt

⅓ cup (75 mL) cold vegan butter, cut into ½-inch (1 cm) cubes

¾ cup (175 mL) unsweetened almond milk, plus extra for brushing the biscuits

3 large fresh peaches, peeled and sliced

2 to 3 cups (500 to 750 mL) coconut whipped topping

¼ cup (60 mL) pure liquid honey or maple syrup

12 sprigs fresh thyme or 6 sprigs fresh lavender

NAKED COCONUT CAKE

Makes one 8-inch (20 cm) round two-layer cake; serves 12 to 14

This cake has become a favourite for birthday parties and special occasions. It is decadent, showy, and bursting at the seams with coconut! Tori has been tweaking this recipe for years since first making it for Jillian's birthday a decade ago. This cake is dense and moist and best served the day it is made. If you do not like icing, skip it and serve the cake with some coconut whipped topping and berries for a less sweet option.

1. MAKE THE COCONUT CAKE Preheat the oven to 350°F (180°C). Grease and flour two 8-inch (20 cm) round cake pans.

2. In a large bowl using a hand-held electric mixer or in a stand mixer fitted with the paddle attachment, cream together the coconut oil and sugar on medium speed until light and fluffy.

3. Add the eggs one at a time, beating well after each addition, and then beat in the vanilla and almond extract.

4. In a medium bowl, sift together the flour, baking powder, baking soda, and salt. Beat the flour mixture into the creamed mixture alternately with the coconut milk, making 2 additions of each. Fold in the shredded coconut.

5. Divide the batter evenly between the prepared pans, spreading it evenly with a rubber spatula. Bake until the cake pulls away from the sides and a toothpick inserted into the centre comes out clean, 40 to 50 minutes. Let the cakes cool in the pans on a rack for 10 minutes. Invert the cakes onto the rack, flip the cakes so they are the right side up, and let cool completely. (The cake layers can be wrapped tightly in plastic wrap and stored in the freezer for up to 2 weeks.)

6. MEANWHILE, MAKE THE ICING Cream the butter in a medium bowl with an electric mixer on medium-high speed until light and fluffy, about 2 minutes.

7. Add the vanilla, almond extract, and icing sugar and beat until it is smooth (it will be thick). Beat in the coconut milk 1 tablespoon (15 mL) at a time until the icing is a spreadable consistency. Transfer half of the icing to a piping bag fitted with a large round tip; reserve the remaining icing.

Coconut Cake

1½ cups (375 mL) coconut oil

2 cups (500 mL) sugar

5 eggs

2 teaspoons (10 mL) pure vanilla extract

1 teaspoon (5 mL) pure almond extract

3 cups (750 mL) all-purpose flour

1 teaspoon (5 mL) baking powder

½ teaspoon (2 mL) baking soda

½ teaspoon (2 mL) salt

1 cup (250 mL) canned full-fat coconut milk

1½ cups (375 mL) unsweetened shredded coconut

1 cup (250 mL) ribbon coconut, for garnish

Icing

1 cup (250 mL) butter or vegan butter

1 teaspoon (5 mL) pure vanilla extract

½ teaspoon (2 mL) pure almond extract

4 cups (1 L) icing sugar, sifted

2 to 4 tablespoons (30 to 60 mL) canned full-fat coconut milk or unsweetened almond milk

Continued . . .

8. Once the cakes are cool, level off the tops with a sharp bread knife, holding it as straight as possible horizontally to create 2 even cake layers. Lightly shake the layers to remove any loose crumbs.

9. Place one layer on a cake stand cut side up. Pipe an even layer of icing on the cake, starting in the middle and working your way in a circular pattern to the edge. Place the other cake layer cut side down on top of the iced layer. Straighten it to ensure that it is perfectly centred over the bottom layer.

10. Add any icing remaining in the piping bag to the reserved icing. Using a straight metal spatula, scoop some icing onto the top of the cake and spread it approximately ¼ to ½ inch (5 mm to 1 cm) thick across the top. Repeat with a small amount of icing on the spatula along the sides of the cake, holding the spatula at a 90-degree angle so that only a small amount of icing stays on the cake, scraping it evenly and smoothly along the edge of the cake and adding more icing when needed.

11. Sprinkle the ribbon coconut evenly on top of the cake. Store, covered, at room temperature for up to 3 days.

DAIRY-FREE: Use vegan butter.

GLUTEN-FREE: Use certified gluten-free coconut.

CHERRY SWEETHEART SLAB PIE

Serves 16 to 20

Slab pies are the way to go for feeding a crowd; less fuss with every bit and more, if you ask us, wow factor than a traditional pie. You can make this pie any day of the year (using any shaped small cookie cutter you want, such as a small star for Christmas), but we love making this heart-adorned version for Valentine's Day entertaining. We've also made it substituting the cherries with frozen sliced strawberries and adding 1 tablespoon (15 mL) of lemon zest and 2 tablespoons (30 mL) of lemon juice to the filling if you're wanting to switch it up. It is not too sweet and is over-the-top delicious served with a scoop of vanilla ice cream or vanilla dairy-free or vegan ice cream. You can easily cut the recipe in half to make one smaller pie if your plans are more intimate. We love how the cut-out hearts finish off the pie crust edges: they look adorable and they cover up any imperfections in the crust.

1. MAKE THE PIE CRUST In a food processor, combine the flour, sugar, and salt; pulse to mix.

2. Sprinkle the shortening and butter on top of the flour mixture. Pulse until the shortening and butter are just incorporated and the butter pieces are the size of peas. Do not overprocess.

3. Drizzle ½ cup (125 mL) of the ice water over the mixture. Pulse until the dough just starts to stick together in clumps, adding 2 to 4 tablespoons (30 to 60 mL) water, 1 tablespoon (15 mL) at a time, if needed. Divide the dough in half, shape into 2 discs, wrap in plastic wrap, and refrigerate for at least 1 hour before rolling it out.

4. MEANWHILE, MAKE THE CHERRY FILLING Combine the cherries, sugar, cornstarch, and vanilla in a large bowl.

5. Preheat the oven to 425°F (220°C).

6. ASSEMBLE THE SLAB PIE On a well-floured work surface, roll one disc of dough into a 18- × 13-inch (46 × 33 cm) rectangle. Transfer the rolled dough to a 15- × 10-inch (40 × 25 cm) jelly roll pan or baking sheet, making sure the dough extends slightly over all sides of the pan. Gently tuck the dough into the corners of the pan.

7. Pour the cherry filling evenly over the pie dough.

Pie Crust

5 cups (1.25 mL) all-purpose flour

4 teaspoons (20 mL) sugar

2 teaspoons (10 mL) salt

1 cup (250 mL) vegetable shortening, cut into chunks

1 cup (250 mL) cold butter or cold vegan butter, cut into ½-inch (1 cm) cubes

½ cup (125 mL) + 2 to 4 tablespoons (30 to 60 mL) ice water

4 teaspoons (20 mL) fresh lemon juice or white vinegar

1 egg, for egg wash (optional)

Cherry Filling

10 cups (2.4 L) fresh or frozen pitted cherries (about 3 pounds/1.4 kg)

½ cup (125 mL) sugar

½ cup (125 mL) cornstarch

2 teaspoons (10 mL) pure vanilla extract

Continued . . .

Cherry Sweetheart Slab Pie continued

8. Roll out the second disc of dough to the same size. Using a small heart-shaped cookie cutter, cut shapes out of the centre of the dough in an even pattern, leaving a 2-inch (5 cm) border around the edges. Set aside the cut-out hearts. You may need to reroll some scraps to make more cut-out hearts if you run short in step 9.

9. Starting at one end, gently roll the dough completely around the rolling pin. Position the exposed edge of the dough at the edge of the pan and carefully unroll the dough to fit over the pie. Using your fingers, press the edges together to form a flattened edge.

10. In a small bowl, whisk the egg with 1 tablespoon (15 mL) water and brush the top of the dough. Arrange the cut-out hearts in a slightly over-lapping fashion around the flattened edge of the pie to form the crust. Place another baking sheet or foil under the pan to catch any drips if the pie filling seeps out a bit and bake until golden brown, 30 to 40 minutes. Cool slightly in the pan before serving. Store covered at room temperature or in the fridge for up to 3 days.

VEGAN: Use vegan butter and omit the egg wash.

DAIRY-FREE: Use vegan butter.

c

d

e

f

BANANA COCONUT CREAM PIE

Makes one 9-inch (23 cm) pie; serves 10 to 12

Banana cream pie meets the tropics in this twist on a classic. We went to Hawaii together with our families and grandparents when we were kids and came back with some of the best memories of our lives, from Granny rolling in the waves and giggling so hard she couldn't get up to us kids holding hands and singing Ukrainian songs at the top of our lungs on the streets of Honolulu. It's probably why Hawaii remains our favourite place to travel. This is a slightly firmer cream pie, with an easy-to-assemble coconut base layered with piles of sliced fresh bananas and a smooth, creamy, and not-too-sweet filling. You can serve it with regular whipped cream if you are not avoiding dairy.

1. MAKE THE COCONUT CRUST Preheat the oven to 350°F (180°C). Spray a 9-inch (23 cm) pie plate with cooking spray.

2. Combine the shredded coconut, coconut milk, coconut oil, vanilla, and salt in a food processor and process for about 30 seconds, until the coconut starts to stick together. Using the back of a large spoon, evenly spread the coconut mixture in the bottom and up the sides of the pie plate.

3. Bake until the crust it is golden brown along the edges, 13 to 15 minutes, rotating halfway through. Set aside to cool completely.

4. MAKE THE BANANA COCONUT CREAM FILLING In a medium, heavy-bottomed saucepan, combine the cornstarch with ½ cup (125 mL) of the coconut milk; whisk until no lumps remain. Add the remaining 2½ cups (625 mL) coconut milk and maple syrup while whisking.

5. Place the saucepan over medium heat and bring the mixture to a boil, stirring constantly with the whisk. Boil for 1 minute (to cook the starch and thicken the mixture), then whisk in the vanilla and remove from the heat.

6. Pour the filling into the crust and let it cool, uncovered (it will slightly dry on the top), 20 to 30 minutes. Once cooled, cover with plastic wrap and refrigerate for at least 4 hours, or until firm.

7. To serve, top with the banana slices and coconut whipped topping. Store covered in the fridge for up to 4 days. The bananas will turn brown if you are storing the pie, so we recommend slicing fresh bananas to top the pie just before serving.

Coconut Crust

2 cups (500 mL) sweetened shredded coconut

3 tablespoons (45 mL) canned full-fat coconut milk

2 tablespoons (30 mL) coconut oil, melted

½ teaspoon (2 mL) pure vanilla extract

⅛ teaspoon (0.5 mL) salt

Banana Coconut Cream Filling

⅓ cup (75 mL) cornstarch

3 cups (750 mL) canned full-fat coconut milk, divided

⅓ cup (75 mL) pure maple syrup or sugar

2 teaspoons (10 mL) pure vanilla extract

2 large bananas, sliced

Coconut whipped topping

GLUTEN-FREE: Use certified gluten-free coconut.

PECAN PUMPKIN PIE

Makes one 10-inch (25 cm) pie; serves 8 to 10

Dessert time at Thanksgiving has always been a bit of a letdown for our aunt Mary and cousin Steph: neither can have gluten. We created this pie so they wouldn't be left out, but we think it's even better than the plain ol' regular pie that we used to serve—and much healthier! Pumpkin pie is traditionally made with evaporated milk, but we highly recommend making it with our Cashew Cream (page 313)—it yields a much richer and smoother filling that was preferred hands down by our crowd. Serve with a dollop of whipped cream or coconut whipped topping.

1. Preheat the oven to 350°F (180°C).

2. MAKE THE PECAN CRUST In a food processor, combine the pecans, oat flour, brown sugar, melted butter, cinnamon, and salt. Pulse until the mixture is finely ground and sticks together well when pressed between your fingers.

3. Tip the pecan mixture into a 10-inch (25 cm) ceramic fluted quiche pan and, using the flat bottom of a glass, press it evenly and firmly onto the bottom and up the sides to form the crust.

4. Bake for 12 minutes, or until the crust looks slightly cooked but not brown. Set aside.

5. MAKE THE PUMPKIN PIE FILLING In a large bowl, combine the pumpkin purée, Cashew Cream, eggs, brown sugar, cinnamon, ginger, nutmeg, cloves, allspice, and salt. Whisk until smooth.

6. Pour the filling into the crust and bake until the centre of the pie is set (a butter knife should come out clean), 30 to 40 minutes. Transfer to a rack and let cool completely. Store, covered, in the fridge for up to 3 days.

Pecan Crust

I cup (250 mL) pecan halves, toasted

I cup (250 mL) oat flour

¼ cup (60 mL) firmly packed brown sugar

⅓ cup (75 mL) butter or vegan butter, melted

½ teaspoon (2 mL) cinnamon

Pinch of salt

Pumpkin Pie Filling

1½ cups (375 mL) pure pumpkin purée (from a 19-ounce/540 mL can)

1¼ cups (300 mL) Cashew Cream (page 313)

2 eggs, well beaten

½ cup (125 mL) firmly packed brown sugar

I teaspoon (5 mL) cinnamon

I teaspoon (5 mL) ground ginger

I teaspoon (5 mL) nutmeg

⅛ teaspoon (0.5 mL) ground cloves

¼ teaspoon (1 mL) ground allspice

¼ teaspoon (1 mL) salt

STICKY APPLE DATE TOFFEE PUDDING

Makes one 8-inch (20 cm) round cake; serves 10 to 12

We created this super-rich dessert for Jillian's mom's birthday one year, and it is now Peggy's all-time favourite dessert. It is decadence on a plate, moist and so incredibly delicious, filled with grated apples, dates, and a perfect amount of spice. For a total treat, serve with vanilla ice cream or dairy-free ice cream, or whipped cream or coconut whipped topping.

1. MAKE THE CAKE Preheat the oven to 350°F (180°C). Grease and flour an 8-inch (20 cm) round cake pan.

2. In a small bowl, combine the dates and boiling water. Set aside to soften for at least 15 minutes, then drain.

3. In a medium bowl, whisk together the flour, baking powder, baking soda, salt, cinnamon, and allspice.

4. In a large bowl, using an electric mixer, beat the butter with the brown sugar on medium speed until light and fluffy. Add the eggs, one at a time, beating well after each addition. Add the dates, the flour mixture, grated apple, and vanilla and fold just until moistened.

5. Scrape the batter into the prepared pan. Bake until the edges are golden brown and pull away from the sides and a toothpick inserted into the centre comes out clean, 45 to 50 minutes.

6. MEANWHILE, MAKE THE TOFFEE SAUCE Combine the cream, brown sugar, butter, and salt in a medium, heavy-bottomed saucepan. Bring to a simmer over medium-low heat, stirring constantly. Remove from the heat.

7. Remove the cake from the oven and cool in the pan on a rack for 5 minutes. Invert the cake onto a cake plate or cake pedestal. Using a chopstick, poke holes all over cake and pour about ½ cup (125 mL) of the warm Toffee Sauce over the cake; let absorb for at least 25 minutes.

8. Just before serving, if desired, arrange the apple slices in a ring pattern on top of the cake. Serve the cake warm with the remaining Toffee Sauce on the side and your favourite topping. Store at room temperature, covered, for up to 4 days.

DAIRY-FREE: Use vegan butter. For the Toffee Sauce, use coconut cream instead of whipping cream. Serve with coconut whipped cream or dairy-free ice cream.

Cake

11 ounces (300 g) Medjool dates, pitted and finely chopped (about 20 dates)

1 cup (250 mL) boiling water

½ cup (125 mL) all-purpose flour

1 teaspoon (5 mL) baking powder

1 teaspoon (5 mL) baking soda

¼ teaspoon (1 mL) salt

1 teaspoon (5 mL) cinnamon

¼ teaspoon (1 mL) ground allspice

½ cup (125 mL) butter or vegan butter, at room temperature

¾ cup (175 mL) firmly packed brown sugar

2 eggs

¾ cup (175 mL) grated peeled apple (Spartan, Gala, or McIntosh)

1 teaspoon (5 mL) pure vanilla extract

1 apple, cored and thinly sliced, for decoration (optional; Ambrosia is best as it resists browning)

Toffee Sauce

¼ teaspoon (1 mL) salt

1 cup (250 mL) whipping (35%) cream or coconut cream

1 cup (250 mL) firmly packed brown sugar

½ cup (125 mL) butter or vegan butter

RHUBARB CRISP

Serves 8 to 10

In northern Alberta, where we grew up, rhubarb grows *everywhere*! We have seen some creative concoctions (ever try rhubarb relish? It's delicious!), but our family favourite is still this old-fashioned rhubarb crisp. It is such a gorgeous dish, with the pink rhubarb peeking through the oats and the perfect amount of sweetness to offset the tart rhubarb. Plus, it's easily adaptable to be both gluten-free and vegan. Serve with a scoop of your favourite vanilla "nice cream" while still slightly warm.

1. Preheat the oven to 350°F (180°C).

2. In a medium bowl, combine the oats, flour, brown sugar, cinnamon, and salt. Stir with a wooden spoon until combined. Drizzle with the melted butter and toss to combine.

3. In a separate medium bowl, combine the rhubarb, white cane sugar, and cornstarch.

4. Scrape the rhubarb mixture into a 12- × 8-inch (3 L) baking dish and spread it evenly. Sprinkle the oat mixture evenly over the rhubarb to cover.

5. Bake until the topping starts to turn golden brown and the rhubarb mixture bubbles, 45 to 50 minutes. Let cool slightly before serving. Store, covered, in the fridge for up to 3 days.

VEGAN: Use vegan butter or coconut oil.

GLUTEN-FREE: Use certified gluten-free rolled oats and replace the all-purpose flour with your favourite gluten-free 1:1 flour blend.

2 cups (500 mL) old-fashioned rolled oats

I cup (250 mL) all-purpose flour

I cup (250 mL) firmly packed brown sugar

1½ teaspoons (7 mL) cinnamon

½ teaspoon (2 mL) salt

¾ cup (175 mL) butter, vegan butter, or coconut oil, melted

8 cups (2 L) diced fresh or frozen rhubarb

½ cup (125 mL) white cane sugar

2 teaspoons (10 mL) cornstarch

MINI CHERRY ALMOND CRUMBLES

Serves 6

Individual-sized desserts are such a sweet way to make anyone feel special, they really class up a dinner party! We tested this recipe using both fresh and frozen cherries with success both ways, which means that this dessert can be made at any time of year. We are head over heels in love with the combination of cherries and almonds (which also happens to make the house smell unbelievable). Serve each crumble topped with a small scoop of vanilla ice cream or dairy-free ice cream, if desired.

1. Preheat the oven to 350°F (180°C). Place six 1-cup (250 mL) ramekins on a baking sheet lined with parchment paper.

2. Combine the cherries, white cane sugar, cornstarch, and almond extract in a medium bowl and stir to combine well. Divide the cherry mixture equally among the ramekins.

3. In a separate medium bowl, combine the oats, flour, almonds, brown sugar, cinnamon, salt, and melted vegan butter; stir to combine. Sprinkle the oat mixture evenly over the cherry-filled ramekins.

4. Bake until the topping is golden brown and the cherries are bubbling, 35 to 45 minutes. Cool slightly before serving.

GLUTEN-FREE: Use certified gluten-free oats. In place of the all-purpose flour, use a gluten-free 1:1 flour blend or oat flour.

4 cups (1 L) pitted fresh or frozen cherries (if using fresh, cut in half)

2 tablespoons (30 mL) white cane sugar

2 teaspoons (10 mL) cornstarch

½ teaspoon (2 mL) pure almond extract

1 cup (250 mL) old-fashioned rolled oats

⅔ cup (150 mL) all-purpose flour

½ cup (125 mL) sliced raw almonds

⅓ cup (75 mL) firmly packed brown sugar

½ teaspoon (2 mL) cinnamon

Pinch of salt

½ cup (125 mL) vegan butter, melted

BLACK BEAN COCONUT BROWNIES

Makes 16 to 20 brownies

Our granny was way ahead of her time. She was making chickpea brownies ages before they were *a thing*. We followed her lead and created a black bean coconut version that is on repeat in our house. It is dense and fudgy, with a perfect sprinkle of coconut on top: nobody will believe it's made with healthy beans! It's also gluten-free (zero flour) and dairy-free and is made in a blender in one easy step: our kind of recipe. We have been told that these brownies taste exceptional with a drizzle of Vegan Caramel Sauce (page 256), in case you were looking to up your brownie game (note that the sauce is not gluten-free).

1. Preheat the oven to 350°F (180°C). Line an 8-inch (2 L) square cake pan or a 9½-inch (24 cm) round baking pan with parchment paper, leaving extra paper to overhang to make it easier to remove the brownies once baked.

2. In a blender, combine the black beans, cocoa powder, sugar, espresso powder, baking powder, salt, eggs, coconut oil, maple syrup, almond milk, and vanilla. Blend until smooth, about 3 minutes.

3. Scrape the batter into the prepared pan, smoothing the top. Sprinkle with the shredded coconut and chocolate chips (if using). Bake until the brownies pull away from the edges of the pan and a toothpick inserted into the centre comes out clean, about 40 minutes.

4. Let cool in the pan on a rack for 20 to 30 minutes. Using the overhanging parchment paper, lift the brownies out of the pan. Cut with a sharp knife. Store, covered, in the fridge for up to 5 days.

VEGAN: Use Flax or Chia Eggs (page 315) instead of eggs. Use dairy-free chocolate.

GLUTEN-FREE: Use certified gluten-free coconut.

NUT-FREE: Use soy milk or your favourite nut-free milk instead of almond milk.

I can (14 ounces/540 mL) black beans, drained and rinsed

½ cup (125 mL) unsweetened cocoa powder

½ cup (125 mL) sugar or coconut sugar

I teaspoon (5 mL) instant espresso powder

I teaspoon (5 mL) baking powder

¼ teaspoon (I mL) salt

2 eggs

¼ cup (60 mL) coconut oil, melted

2 tablespoons (30 mL) pure maple syrup

2 tablespoons (30 mL) unsweetened almond milk

I teaspoon (5 mL) pure vanilla extract

⅓ cup (75 mL) unsweetened shredded coconut

⅓ cup (75 mL) semi-sweet chocolate chips or chunks (optional)

CHEWY CHOCOLATE CHIP COOKIES

Makes 12 to 15 large cookies

If you have been on the hunt for the perfect chocolate chip cookie recipe (and who hasn't, quite frankly), look no further. You have found *the one*. Our gal Mackenzie took it upon herself to create the perfect chocolate chip cookie and has been sweet enough to share it with the world here. This cookie is crispy yet moist and chewy, sweet and salty, and completely vegan—not that you would ever know. If you're trying to decide between vegan butter and coconut oil, we tested with both: the vegan butter was a slight favourite, but they were both absolutely delicious.

1. Preheat the oven to 350°F (180°C). Line a baking sheet with parchment paper.

2. In a medium bowl, cream together the brown sugar and vegan butter using an electric mixer on medium speed until the mixture is light and fluffy. Add the almond milk and vanilla and beat until combined.

3. In a separate medium bowl, whisk together the flour, baking powder, baking soda, and sea salt. Add the flour mixture to the creamed mixture and beat until just combined. Avoid overmixing. Fold in the chopped dark chocolate.

4. Using a cookie scoop or your hands, form the dough into balls slightly smaller than golf balls and place them on the prepared baking sheet 2 inches (5 cm) apart. Using the back of a fork, lightly pat down each cookie. Lightly sprinkle cookies with flaky sea salt.

5. Bake until light golden brown, 10 to 14 minutes. Cool slightly on the baking sheet and enjoy. Store in a resealable container at room temperature for up to 7 days or in the freezer for up to 2 months.

NUT-FREE: Use soy milk.

1 cup (250 mL) firmly packed brown sugar

½ cup (125 mL) vegan butter or coconut oil

¼ cup (60 mL) unsweetened almond milk or soy milk

2 teaspoons (10 mL) pure vanilla extract

1½ cups (375 mL) all-purpose flour

1 teaspoon (5 mL) baking powder

1 teaspoon (5 mL) baking soda

1 teaspoon (5 mL) sea salt

1¼ cups (300 mL) chopped dairy-free dark chocolate

2 teaspoons (10 mL) flaky sea salt

BUTTERLESS BUTTER TART SQUARES

Makes 16 to 20 squares

Butter tart squares have been a staple on our Christmas treat platter ever since Tori started baking them as a kid. Everyone likes butter tarts, but why on earth fuss with making individual tarts when you can throw the ingredients in one pan and still have the same delicious taste in a jiffy? Of course, the original recipe had twice the amount of sugar and loads of butter, eggs, and real cream. This lightened-up vegan version is still decadent but not nearly as sweet. We served these to unsuspecting guinea pigs and the squares disappeared in minutes! You can buy milled or ground flaxseed at most grocery or health food stores or you can grind whole flaxseeds in seconds if you have a coffee or spice grinder.

1. Preheat the oven to 350°F (180°C). Grease an 8-inch (2.5 L) square cake pan and line it with parchment paper, leaving extra paper to overhang to make it easier to remove the squares once baked.

2. MAKE THE BASE In a medium bowl, cream the vegan butter with the brown sugar using an electric mixer on medium speed. Add the flour and salt and beat until the flour is well incorporated. The mixture will look a bit dry.

3. Press the mixture firmly and evenly into the bottom of the prepared pan using your fingers or the flat bottom of a glass. Bake for 12 to 13 minutes, until the crust is set (it will not look brown at this stage). Remove from the oven.

4. MAKE THE FILLING In a small cup or bowl, stir together the water and flaxseed. Let sit for 5 minutes.

5. In a medium bowl, combine the flaxseed mixture, brown sugar, vegan butter, coconut cream, flour, and vanilla. Beat with an electric mixer on medium speed until well incorporated and creamy. Stir in the raisins and pecans (if using). Pour the filling over the prepared base. Bake until the top bubbles and the edges are golden brown, about 20 minutes.

6. Let cool completely in the pan. Remove the squares from the pan, using the parchment paper to lift them out, place on a cutting board, and cut into squares with a large, sharp knife. Store in a resealable container in the fridge for up to 1 week or in the freezer for up to 1 month.

NUT-FREE: Skip the nuts.

Base

⅓ cup (75 mL) vegan butter

¼ cup (60 mL) firmly packed brown sugar

1 cup (250 mL) all-purpose flour

¼ teaspoon (1 mL) salt

Filling

¼ cup (60 mL) water

2 tablespoons (30 mL) milled or ground flaxseed

½ cup (125 mL) firmly packed brown sugar

⅓ cup (75 mL) vegan butter

2 tablespoons (30 mL) coconut cream (see Tip)

1 tablespoon (15 mL) all-purpose flour

1 teaspoon (5 mL) pure vanilla extract

1 cup (250 mL) raisins

½ cup (125 mL) chopped raw pecans or walnuts (optional)

TIP: You can purchase coconut cream or simply refrigerate a can of full-fat coconut milk overnight. When ready to use, open the can and scoop out the solid white coconut cream on the top. Store the remaining coconut cream and coconut water in the fridge for up to 6 days.

RASPBERRY ALMOND OAT BARS

Makes 24 bars

Raspberries and almonds were made for each other, and these bars are proof! You can use fresh or frozen raspberries in this recipe, which means you can enjoy these delicious bars all year round. The filling is thickened with healthy chia seeds for an extra dose of omega-3 fats, protein, and fibre, and these bars are packed with nutritious almonds in every shape and form. The glaze dresses the bars up and adds a touch of extra sweetness. Serve these at a picnic, at tea, or for a sweet touch to your brunch table for guests.

1. MAKE THE RASPBERRY CHIA FILLING Mash together the raspberries, chia seeds, sugar, and vanilla in a medium bowl. Let sit for at least 2 hours or overnight in the fridge.

2. Preheat the oven to 350°F (180°C). Grease a 13- × 9-inch (3.5 L) cake pan and line with parchment paper, leaving extra paper to overhang to make it easier to remove the bars once baked.

3. MAKE THE ALMOND OAT CRUMBLE Place the almonds in a food processor and pulse until the finely ground. Empty them into a large bowl. Add the oats, oat flour, brown sugar, melted vegan butter, almond extract, vanilla, and salt. Mix well. Set aside ¾ cup (175 mL) of the oat mixture in a small bowl.

4. Transfer the remaining oat mixture to the food processor. Add the almond butter and process until the mixture sticks together. Scrape into the prepared baking dish and evenly and firmly press the mixture onto the bottom of the pan using the flat bottom of a glass. Bake until the crust looks slightly cooked but not brown, about 10 minutes.

5. Add the sliced almonds to the reserved oat mixture and stir to combine.

6. Spread the Raspberry Chia Filling evenly over the prepared base, then sprinkle the almond and oat mixture evenly on top. Bake until the top is lightly browned, 35 to 45 minutes. Let cool completely.

Raspberry Chia Filling

3 cups (750 mL) fresh or thawed frozen raspberries

6 tablespoons (90 mL) chia seeds

¼ cup (60 mL) sugar

½ teaspoon (2 mL) pure vanilla extract

Almond Oat Crumble

1 cup (250 mL) whole raw almonds, toasted

2 cups (500 mL) old-fashioned rolled oats

½ cup (125 mL) oat flour

½ cup (125 mL) firmly packed brown sugar

⅔ cup (150 mL) vegan butter or coconut oil, melted

½ teaspoon (2 mL) pure almond extract

½ teaspoon (2 mL) pure vanilla extract

¼ teaspoon (1 mL) salt

¼ cup (60 mL) natural almond butter

½ cup (125 mL) sliced raw almonds

Continued . . .

Raspberry Almond Oat Bars continued

7. MEANWHILE, MAKE THE ALMOND GLAZE Stir together the icing sugar, 1 tablespoon (15 mL) of the almond milk, and almond extract in a small bowl, adding extra almond milk to make the glaze just thin enough to drizzle.

8. Remove the cooled bars from the pan, using the parchment paper to lift them out, and place on a cutting board. Using a small spoon, drizzle the bars lightly with the Almond Glaze, then cut into bars using a large, sharp knife. Store in a resealable container at room temperature for up to 3 days or in the freezer for up to 2 weeks.

GLUTEN-FREE: Use certified gluten-free oats and oat flour.

Almond Glaze

¾ cup (175 mL) icing sugar

I to 2 tablespoons (15 to 30 mL) unsweetened almond milk

¼ teaspoon (I mL) pure almond extract

AUNTY MARY'S BANANA BREAD

Makes 1 loaf

Everybody needs a good banana bread recipe in their repertoire to use up all those overripe bananas that every house has! Tori started making this banana bread when she was thirteen, and it has been a family favourite ever since. The original recipe was from our Aunty Mary, handed down through generations. Tori has tweaked it a bit to reduce the sugar and fat, and we think it tastes just as good! The kids love this with chocolate (big surprise), and the adults prefer it with nuts, so we usually mix up two loaves to make everyone happy. You can easily make muffins instead; bake for 15 to 20 minutes or until a toothpick inserted into the centre comes out clean.

1. Preheat the oven to 350°F (180°C). Grease and lightly flour an 8- × 4-inch (1.5 L) loaf pan (or line the greased pan with parchment paper).

2. In a medium bowl, whisk together the all-purpose flour, whole wheat flour, baking powder, and salt. Set aside.

3. In a large bowl, using an electric mixer (or a stand mixer fitted with the paddle attachment), beat the butter with the sugar on medium-high speed until light and fluffy, about 2 minutes. Add the eggs, one at a time, beating well after each addition. Beat for 1 minute more, scraping down the sides of the bowl as needed. Add the bananas and the vanilla and beat again until fully incorporated.

4. In a small saucepan or in the microwave, heat the milk until it starts to bubble. Add the baking soda to the milk. (Caution: it will foam and expand, so make sure your saucepan or bowl can accommodate the extra volume!) Add this to the batter along with the flour mixture and beat for another 1 minute or until just combined, scraping the sides of the bowl as needed. Fold in the walnuts or chocolate chips (if using).

½ cup (125 mL) all-purpose flour

½ cup (125 mL) whole wheat flour

1 teaspoon (5 mL) baking powder

¼ teaspoon (1 mL) salt

⅓ cup (75 mL) butter or vegan butter, at room temperature

½ cup (125 mL) sugar or coconut sugar

2 eggs

2 very ripe bananas, mashed

1 teaspoon (5 mL) pure vanilla extract

2 tablespoons (30 mL) 2% milk or unsweetened almond milk

1 teaspoon (5 mL) baking soda

½ cup (125 mL) chopped raw walnuts or pecans, or dark chocolate chips (optional)

Continued . . .

5. Scrape the batter into the loaf pan, smooth the top with a rubber spatula or large spoon, and bake until a toothpick inserted into the centre comes out clean, 30 to 40 minutes. Let cool in the pan on a rack for 10 minutes before turning the cake out of the pan. Let cool completely before slicing (if you can resist!). Store, covered, at room temperature for up to 3 days or in the freezer for up to 1 month.

DAIRY-FREE: Use vegan butter. Use unsweetened almond milk instead of milk and dairy-free chocolate chips (if using).

NUT-FREE: Use 2% milk or your favourite nut-free milk. Use ¾ cup (175 mL) fresh or frozen (unthawed) blueberries instead of nuts.

DRINKS

OKANAGAN PEACH SLUSHIES

Serves 2

When the peaches are falling off the trees in the heat of summer, you will find us filling our freezers with sliced ripe peaches and whipping out our blenders to make these beauties. A peach overload problem is the very best kind of problem to have, and friends, these refreshing drinks are the solution.

1. In a blender, combine the peaches, rum, peach schnapps, and ice. Blend until smooth. Divide between 2 champagne flutes or martini glasses.

2. Stir together the raspberry liqueur and red wine. Pour half the mixture over each glass and serve.

2 cups (500 mL) frozen sliced peeled peaches

2 ounces white rum

2 ounces peach schnapps

1 cup (250 mL) ice

1 ounce raspberry liqueur

1 ounce dry red wine (we use sangiovese)

STRAWBERRY ROSÉ-ARITA

Serves 6

Frozen strawberries are kissed by pretty rosé to make these thirst-quenching, perfectly sweet drinks. The lemon juice really brightens up the flavours of this simple drink with just a few ingredients thrown into a blender to make a beautiful summer beverage for a crowd in a matter of seconds. Because who wants to spend their summer afternoons slaving away in the kitchen making fancy drinks? That poolside lounger is calling your name!

1. In a high-speed blender, combine the strawberries, lemon juice, simple syrup, rosé, and ice. Blend on high until smooth, 1 to 2 minutes.

2. Serve in wine glasses or tumblers with a sprig of mint.

4 cups (1 L) frozen sliced strawberries

3 tablespoons (45 mL) fresh lemon juice

2 tablespoons (30 mL) simple syrup (see Tip)

1 bottle (26 ounces/750 mL) rosé wine

2 cups (500 mL) ice cubes

6 sprigs fresh mint

TIP: To make simple syrup, combine equal amounts sugar and water in a small saucepan and simmer until the sugar has dissolved. Let cool, then store in a covered container in the fridge for up to 2 months.

a

b

c

d

e

f

CHERRY SUNSET

Serves 2

Summer sunsets in the Okanagan are pure magic. A soft haze sets in the valley at the same time as the vineyards and orchards are warmed with the amber glow of the sun slowly sinking behind the mountains. This drink reminds us of those balmy hazy nights. When carefully poured, it mirrors the sunset in the yummiest way possible. Cherries and almonds are a match made in heaven in this oh-so pretty and lightly sweetened cocktail, perfect for those hot summer evenings when the cherry trees are at their prime. The amaretto gives it an unexpected twist that really complements the ripe cherries. The egg white or aquafaba is optional: it makes the drink frothy, but can be left out.

1. Moisten the rim of 2 tall glasses with water and dip the rim in the sugar to coat.

2. Divide the chopped cherries between the rimmed glasses and fill each glass with ice.

3. Put the pineapple juice, amaretto, and rum, and egg white (if using) in a mason jar or shaker. Seal the jar or shaker and shake it back and forth about 20 times. Divide between the glasses. Top with a splash of club soda and serve.

VEGAN: Use aquafaba.

2 tablespoons (30 mL) sugar, for rimming the glasses

¼ cup (60 mL) pitted and finely chopped fresh cherries

Ice

¾ cup (175 mL) pineapple juice

2 ounces amaretto

2 ounces white rum or tequila

1 egg white or 2 tablespoons (30 mL) aquafaba (canned chickpea liquid; optional)

Club soda

COCONUT LEMONADE

Serves 6 to 8

Nothing rivals homemade lemonade. Jillian created this crazy-good version that gets a creamy tropical makeover! Reminiscent of a lemon creamsicle in a glass, it's creamy enough to feel indulgent but zippy enough to feel refreshing. You can add a splash of vodka to the lemonade, if you wish—we won't judge!

1. MAKE THE SIMPLE SYRUP Combine the sugar, water, and lemon zest in a small saucepan and simmer until the sugar has dissolved. Let cool completely and strain through a fine sieve to remove the zest before using.

2. MAKE THE LEMONADE Pour the coconut cream into a blender and blend until smooth.

3. In a large pitcher, combine the blended coconut cream, lemon juice, ½ cup (125 mL) of the Simple Syrup, and the water. Stir well to combine. Taste and add more Simple Syrup if you like a sweeter lemonade.

4. To serve, fill each glass with ice, add a couple slices of lemon, and fill the glasses with the lemonade.

Simple Syrup

½ cup (125 mL) sugar

½ cup (125 mL) water

Zest of 1 lemon

Lemonade

½ can (7 ounces/200 mL) coconut cream

1 cup (250 mL) fresh lemon juice (from about 6 lemons)

4 cups (1 L) water

Ice

Lemon slices, for serving

GRAPEFRUIT JALAPEÑO MARGARITA

Serves 4

These super-yummy margaritas are insanely easy to make and always a hit! Do not be scared off by the egg white (or aquafaba); it makes the cocktail smooth and slightly creamy. Many bars serve their cocktails this way, and once you try it, you will never go back. Serve these on the rocks in large tumbler glasses or traditional margarita glasses to feel like you are sipping it in Mexico. Yum!

1. Moisten the rim of tumbler glasses or margarita glasses with the juice of 1 lime and dip the rim in the Himalayan pink salt to coat.

2. In a large drink container with a lid, combine the grapefruit juice, pineapple juice, tequila, triple sec, the remaining lime juice, jalapeño, and egg white. Shake with all your might! (If you do not have such a container, combine everything in a pitcher and stir well.)

3. Pour into glasses filled with ice.

Juice of 2 limes, divided

Himalayan pink salt, for rimming the glasses

3 cups (750 mL) pink grapefruit juice

1 cup (250 mL) pineapple juice

½ cup (125 mL) tequila

1 ounce triple sec

½ jalapeño pepper, seeded and finely sliced into rounds

1 egg white or 2 tablespoons (30 mL) aquafaba (canned chickpea liquid)

Ice

VEGAN: Use aquafaba.

ELDERFLOWER GIN AND TONIC

Serves 1

Tori's favourite drink (other than wine) is a gin and tonic. If you are looking to take your G and T game to a new level, look no further. This pretty and classy drink is taken up a notch with elderflower liqueur and infused with a whisper of ripe Bartlett pear—so refreshing and fragrant! It looks stunning garnished with an edible white flower. We serve this at the start of fall, when the weather is still warm enough to justify an iced beverage and the pears are starting to fall off the tree. We have some gorgeous local small-batch gins in the Okanagan. Try out your own local gins to find one that makes this drink extra special!

1. Pour the gin and elderflower liqueur into a tall glass and stir.

2. Add the ice and tonic water, and top up with a splash of club soda. Garnish with a thin slice of Bartlett pear and serve.

2 ounces gin

1 ounce elderflower liqueur (such as St-Germain)

Ice

⅔ cup (150 mL) tonic water

Splash of club soda

Thin slice of fresh semi-firm Bartlett pear

SAMMY'S MULLED WINE

Serves 6 to 8

When our cousin Sammy was living in Austria with her husband, Dustin, and new baby, Hayden, Jilly paid them a visit one winter. Rumour has it they drank their weight in Glühwein (mulled wine), after which Jilly created this epic recipe so that we could enjoy it back in Canada. We get enough snow, so we deserve it! This is the best version of mulled wine we have ever had (not to toot our own horn) and is perfect for cold winter nights after skiing or skating. We hope you love it, too!

¾ cup (175 mL) sugar, more for rimming the mugs

¾ cup (175 mL) water

1 large orange, halved crosswise

1 large grapefruit, halved crosswise

1 lemon

10 whole cloves

10 whole star anise

2 cinnamon sticks

1 bottle (26 ounces/750 mL) dry red wine (we use cabernet merlot)

½ cup (125 mL) spiced rum

Cinnamon sticks or orange slices, for garnish

1. In a large pot, bring the sugar and water to a boil.

2. Meanwhile, juice one orange half and one grapefruit half into a small bowl. Using a vegetable peeler, peel the lemon rind (yellow part only) into long strips. Press the cloves into the rind of the unjuiced orange half and add it to the boiling water. Add the lemon peel, orange and grapefruit juices, star anise, and cinnamon sticks. Simmer for 5 minutes.

3. Reduce the heat to low and add the red wine and spiced rum. Simmer gently for 5 minutes. Remove from the heat and strain into a clean pot. Keep warm.

4. Pour ½ inch (1 cm) of water into a shallow dish. Fill a similar dish with ½ inch (1 cm) sugar. Dip the rim of each mug in the water, then dip it into the sugar to coat the rim.

5. Divide the warm mulled wine among the mugs. Garnish with a cinnamon stick or a slice of orange and serve.

a

b

c

d

VEGAN EGGNOG

Serves 4

The first sign of eggnog hitting the store shelves is our cue to pull out the Christmas lights and fire up the Bing Crosby. We wanted to create a vegan version that is so much lighter on the calories but doesn't compromise on taste, and this is it. We left rum out of the ingredients, but feel free to add (quantities at your discretion!). Happy Holidays!

1. In a blender, combine the vanilla soy milk, coconut milk, maple syrup, cinnamon, cloves, and nutmeg. Blend until smooth and frothy.

2. Pour into glasses filled with ice. Garnish with a sprinkle of cinnamon and a cinnamon stick and serve.

3 cups (750 mL) vanilla soy milk

1 cup (250 mL) canned full-fat coconut milk

¼ cup (60 mL) pure maple syrup

½ teaspoon (2 mL) cinnamon, more for garnish

⅛ teaspoon (0.5 mL) ground cloves

½ teaspoon (2 mL) nutmeg

Ice

4 cinnamon sticks, for garnish

VEGAN SUBSTITUTES

CASHEW CREAM

Makes 4 cups (1 L)

Cashew cream is an absolute staple in any plant-based cooking. It is so creamy, it's easy to make, and it requires zero straining (unlike most other nut milks). If you find this too thick, simply blend in a bit more water. Be sure to use raw cashews, not roasted ones. If you are short on time, you can use a quick-soak method instead of soaking the nuts overnight: pour boiling water over the cashews, cover, let sit for 30 minutes, drain, rinse, and you are ready to go! Just don't soak them longer than 12 hours or they will be bitter.

3 cups (750 mL) raw cashews

3 cups (500 mL) water

1. Soak the cashews in water for at least 4 hours or overnight (up to 12 hours) in the fridge. Drain and rinse before using.

2. In a high-speed blender, blend the drained cashews and the water on high speed until very smooth, 2 to 3 minutes. Store in a resealable container in the fridge for up to 5 days.

VEGAN PARM

Makes 1¼ cups (300 mL)

We love how simple it is to make your own vegan parmesan! Although this will not melt like traditional Parmesan cheese, it does add a similar flavour. Try it sprinkled on top of Garden Bolognese (page 158) or Rosemary Polenta Fries (page 111).

1 cup (250 mL) raw cashews

¼ cup (60 mL) nutritional yeast

¾ teaspoon (4 mL) sea salt

¼ teaspoon (1 mL) garlic powder

1. In a mini food processor, pulse the cashews, nutritional yeast, salt, and garlic powder until finely ground, 20 to 40 seconds. Store in a resealable container at room temperature for up to 3 months.

ALMOND TRUFFLE PARM

Makes ¾ cup (175 mL)

This may not be a dead ringer for Parmesan cheese, but we'll take it any day over the real deal! Sprinkle this on pasta, roasted veggies—the options are endless.

½ cup (125 mL) ground raw almonds

¼ cup (60 mL) nutritional yeast

1 teaspoon (5 mL) white truffle oil

½ teaspoon (2 mL) sea salt

1. Stir together the almonds, nutritional yeast, white truffle oil, and salt in a small bowl. Store in a resealable container at room temperature for up to 3 months.

VEGAN SOUR CREAM

Makes 2 cups (500 mL)

This makes a rather thick "sour cream." If you prefer a thinner sour cream, simply add a bit of water and blend again.

1. Soak the cashews in water for at least 4 hours or overnight (up to 12 hours) in the fridge. Drain and rinse before using (see Tip).

2. In a high-speed blender, combine the drained cashews, water, lemon juice, cider vinegar, and salt. Blend on high speed until smooth. Store in a resealable container in the fridge for up to 5 days.

3 cups (750 mL) raw cashews

½ cup (125 mL) water

1 tablespoon (15 mL) fresh lemon juice

2 teaspoons (10 mL) apple cider vinegar

½ teaspoon (2 mL) salt

TIP: The overnight soak works best, but if you don't have time to soak the cashews for several hours (or forgot), you can use the quick soak method: soak them in boiling water for 30 minutes, then drain and rinse.

FLAX OR CHIA EGG

Replacement for 1 egg

You can use flax or chia eggs in most baking. The baked product is usually much denser, but it typically works and doesn't alter the flavour!

1. Stir together the ground flaxseed or chia seeds and water in a small bowl and let sit for 5 to 10 minutes before using.

1 tablespoon (15 mL) ground flaxseed or ground chia seeds

3 tablespoons (45 mL) water

VEGAN FETA

Makes about 2 cups (500 mL) crumbled "feta"

We experimented with all sorts of vegan feta concoctions before settling on this one. It is made creamy by the Cashew Cream (page 313), and it's briny and zippy just like the real deal. It will not melt the same way as feta does, but it's a great substitute for feta in any uncooked use, such as salads. Be sure to press the tofu: the longer it is pressed, the more liquid will be extracted and the more brine (a.k.a. flavour) will be soaked up.

1 package (12 ounces/350 g) extra-firm tofu, drained

1 cup (250 mL) Cashew Cream (page 313)

Juice of 1 lemon

½ cup (125 mL) extra-virgin olive oil

½ cup (125 mL) water

2 tablespoons (30 mL) salt

1½ teaspoons (7 mL) sugar

1. Press the tofu by placing it between 2 sheets of paper towel, then sandwich it between 2 plates. Place a heavy object such as a stack of books on top; refrigerate for at least 2 hours or up to 1 day.

2. Cut the pressed tofu into ½-inch (1 cm) cubes.

3. In a dish large enough to hold all the tofu snugly, combine the Cashew Cream, lemon juice, olive oil, water, salt, and sugar. Whisk well. Add the tofu and toss to combine. The tofu should be submerged in the brine (if not, transfer it to a different bowl). Cover and refrigerate overnight. Store in a resealable container in the fridge for up to 7 days.

SMOKY TOFU BACON

Serves 2 to 4

One of the biggest things people miss on a plant-based diet is bacon. This vegan version uses smoked tofu and does a darned good job of mimicking the real deal. It tastes incredible on Captain's Kale Caesar Salad (page 131) or on a vegan BLT. You can cut the tofu into thin strips or into cubes as indicated in the recipe, depending what you'll be using it for.

1. Cut the tofu into ¼-inch (5 mm) cubes.

2. Place the tofu in a small frying pan and add the olive oil, maple syrup, and soy sauce. Cook over medium-low heat until the tofu is crispy, about 5 minutes, stirring and turning occasionally. Serve immediately.

1 package (7½ ounces/210 g) smoked extra-firm tofu

4 teaspoons (20 mL) extra-virgin olive oil

1 tablespoon (15 mL) pure maple syrup

1 tablespoon (15 mL) soy sauce or tamari

GLUTEN-FREE: Use gluten-free soy sauce or tamari.

Thank You from the Bottom of Our Hearts

Thank you to all the amazing people who helped bring this book to life. To our incredible family (including our men, Justin and Charles, and our parents) for supporting us in all our crazy adventures; all the wonderful people who tirelessly tested recipes (sometimes over and over again, ahem), Michele St. André, Wendy Solway, Diane Carlson, and Melissa Pasutto; our agent, Tyler Evans, for making this happen; our talented photographer, Janis Nicolay; our editor, Andrea Magyar; and of course the ladies on the team who absolutely killed it on the recipe shoot days (and were ready to kill us in turn, haha . . . so much work!)—Shay Merritt, Mackenzie Dempsey, Mindy Crawford, and Brea Laurin, we love you!

Thank you to the following companies who supplied ingredients and the beautiful props that appear in the book:

Wine: Sandhill Wines (www.sandhillwines.com)

Market baskets and antiques: Dreamy Whites: French Farmhouse Inspired Living (www.dreamywhitesonline.com)

Assorted plates and kitchen props: The Cross (www.thecrossdesign.com)

Garden party and seafood bake décor: Yuriko and Eric Larson (the sweetest people on earth), Vintage Origami (www.vintageorigami.com)

Index